engage

C000271710

The Bible is home to some tru~~ly awesome~~
12 of **engage** we look at two of them — Ruth's heartwarming
love story, and the titanic royal struggle between Saul and
David. We also see what the Bible says about life after death,
living God's way and facing pressure as a Christian.

✱ **DAILY READINGS** Each day's
page throws you into the Bible, to
get you handling, questioning and
exploring God's message to you —
encouraging you to act on it and talk
to God more in prayer.

THIS ISSUE: Get all mushy with
Ruth; tackle a big equation in
Titus; search for the perfect king in **1
Samuel;** locate God's great city with
Isaiah; and take the pressure in **Acts.**

✱ **REAL LIVES** True stories,
revealing God at work in people's
lives. This time — **we see a life
going nowhere turned around.**

✱ **TAKE IT FURTHER** If you're
hungry for more at the end of an
engage page, turn to the **Take it
further** section to dig deeper.

✱ **STUFF** Articles on stuff relevant
to the lives of young Christians.
This issue: **What the Bible says
about abortion.**

✱ **ESSENTIAL** Articles on the
basics we really need to know about
God, the Bible and Christianity.
This issue, we ask the question:
What's this grace thing all about?

✱ **TOOLBOX** is full of tools
to help you understand the Bible.
This issue we see **how the Bible's
words can affect the way we feel.**

✱ **TRICKY** tackles those mind-
bendingly tricky questions that
confuse us all, as well as stuff our
friends bombard us with. This time:
Is there really life after death?

**All of us who work on engage are
passionate to see the Bible at
work in people's lives. Do you
want God's word to have an
impact on your life? Then open
your Bible, and start on the first
engage study right now...**

HOW TO USE engage

1 Set a time you can read the Bible every day

2 Find a place where you can be quiet and think

3 Grab your Bible, pen and a notebook

4 Ask God to help you understand what you read

5 Read the day's verses with engage, taking time to think about it

6 Pray about what you've read

BIBLE STUFF
We use the NIV Bible version, so you might find it's the best one to use with engage. If the notes say **"Ruth 1 v 14–18"**, look up Ruth in the contents page at the front of your Bible. It'll tell you which page the book starts on. Find chapter 1 of Ruth, and then verse 14 of chapter 1 (the verse numbers are the tiny ones). Then start reading. Simple.

In this issue...

DAILY READINGS

Ruth: God's big love story

Titus: Getting it right

1 Samuel: Long live the king

Isaiah: God's perfect city

Acts: Under pressure

ARTICLES

TRICKY
Is there life after death? 12

STUFF
Abortion 26

ESSENTIAL
Amazing grace 40

REAL LIVES
A changed life 58

TOOLBOX
Tone and feel 78

ENGAGE IS LOVINGLY BROUGHT TO YOU BY

Romantic writers: Martin Cole Cassie Martin Carl Laferton
                    Jim Overton Helen Thorne
Gorgeous design: Steve Devane
Pretty proof-readers: Anne Woodcock Richard John
Starry-eyed editor: Martin Cole (martin@thegoodbook.co.uk)

Ruth

God's big love story

Imagine your life edited into a 90-minute movie. In which section of the rental store might you find it? Comedy? Romance? Thriller? The chances are, the true story of your everyday life wouldn't break records at the box office. Real life isn't often like the movies. You can't edit out the dull bits and the plot is hard to follow.

That's why it's great to know there's another bigger story being told. God is steering the world through its dramas to a glorious climax. However entertaining our lives turn out to be, what matters is that we fully take up our part in His story.

The story of Ruth wouldn't be out of place on the big screen. It's got it all — tragedy, romance, drama — and even a happy ending. (Why not read it through like a novel before starting the studies?) But God's big story is also in view. The events described are more than just random happenings to ordinary people. Heaven's King is directing the details of their days. Over the next 8 studies, follow Ruth's story carefully, keeping these key questions in mind:

- How do her experiences and choices compare with mine?
- How has God stepped directly into the chapters of my life?
- Am I living my life like Ruth, to play my part in His plot?

Although God has a plan, there is a sense in which your life remains unwritten. The choices you haven't yet made will shape the story ahead. Let Ruth inspire you to face every episode with faith.

3

1   Who do you think you are?

Imagine life as a refugee. Imagine rolling into a town with no home or mates. Imagine just trying to survive where you don't know the language or customs. Imagine yourself in Naomi's shoes.

👁 Read Ruth 1 v 1–5

ENGAGE YOUR BRAIN

▷ *Why did they leave Bethlehem in the first place?*

▷ *Why was Moab a weird place to run to? (see Judges 3 v 14)*

In their 10 years away, Naomi's family had been hit by multiple tragedies. As if losing her husband wasn't enough, her two sons were taken too. Whatever is to come in her story, it's clear Naomi's past is no picnic.

👁 Read Ruth 1 v 6–13

▷ *Where does the conversation in v8–13 take place? (v7)*

▷ *What are Naomi's hopes for her daughters-in-law? (v8–9)*

▷ *How does she view their prospects if they follow her?*

In many ways, Naomi talks sense. Two foreign widows couldn't expect to get the pick of the available Jewish boys. But there's a hint that her logic has been coloured by her tragic past: Why stick with me? God's against me. (v11, 13)

PRAY ABOUT IT

Have tough times affected your confidence in God? Tell Him about your lowest moments. Then thank Him that circumstances don't change His death-defying love (John 3 v 16).

THE BOTTOM LINE

Even in your lowest moments, don't forget God's great love for you.

➔ TAKE IT FURTHER

For more, turn to page 110.

2 | Clinging on

"It just didn't work out." That's a common verdict on a failed romance. But is that it? Does love just sometimes run out of gas whether we like it or not, or can we keep it moving?

👁 Read Ruth 1 v 14–18

ENGAGE YOUR BRAIN

▶ What pulls Orpah back to Moab (according to Naomi)? (v15)

▶ In contrast, what parts of Naomi's future does Ruth promise to share? (v16–17)

▶ What part of Ruth's character convinces Naomi to stop persuading? (v18)

THINK IT THROUGH

Because life is unpredictable, the idea of being totally committed to anyone or anything for life can seem extreme. But Ruth, not thinking of herself, and knowing her responsibility to God, holds nothing back.

▶ Do you show that type of determination in your love?

👁 Read verses 19–22

▶ What kind of welcome do they receive in Bethlehem?

▶ Naomi means "pleasant". What words in her speech mean the opposite?

▶ What hope is hinted at in v22?

Naomi's friends barely recognise her. Her 10-year ordeal has clearly left its mark. If Naomi is still clinging to the Lord, it's only by her fingernails. But the author wants us to know, it's not over yet.

GET ON WITH IT

▶ Who do you know who's running on empty?

▶ How might you encourage them today to cling to the God who is always good?

THE BOTTOM LINE

For as high as the heavens are above the earth, so great is his love for those who fear him (Psalm 103 v 11).

➡ TAKE IT FURTHER

Cling on and go to page 110.

3 | Don't just sit there!

"It's Not Fair!" It's easy to feel that God does exciting things for others but never for you. Is it possible we need a change to our attitudes and actions?

👁 Read Ruth 2 v 1–13

ENGAGE YOUR BRAIN

▷ *What attitude does Ruth hope to find among the harvesters? (v2)*
▷ *In what ways does Boaz demonstrate just that attitude?*
▷ *What does Boaz expect God to do and why? (v11, 12)*

THINK IT THROUGH

Ruth's mopping up plan is not as cheeky as it seems on the surface. God's law commanded harvesters to be "deliberately careless" — leaving leftovers for poor foreigners. Even in simply receiving what she's entitled to, Ruth is experiencing the simple benefits of her choice to make Naomi's God her God (1 v 16).

👁 Read Ruth 2 v 14–16

▷ *In what way has Boaz exceeded Naomi's expectations and rights? (v14)*
▷ *How does Boaz add to God's basic allowance? (v15–16)*

Ruth's optimistic outlook and humble hard work are a far cry from Naomi's self pity of chapter 1. As a result she starts to experience "over-the-top" favour, showing that God doesn't limit His care for the poor to just survival necessities. It also seems that Boaz is starting to take a shine to Ruth. (Try reading verses 8 and 14 over a romantic movie soundtrack.) God is blessing Ruth by meeting more than her dietary requirements!

GET ON WITH IT

What do you really need? Tell God about it today! Now follow Ruth's simple action plan, showing you trust God to provide.

1. Think about others too. Who can you work alongside who has the same need? (v2)
2. Be bold but humble. Who can you ask respectfully to help you? (v7)
3. Work hard. What effort can you put in towards your target? (v7)

➔ TAKE IT FURTHER

Get up and go to page 110.

4 | Hold on to hope

What a difference a day makes. What might be different by this time tomorrow? The truth is, whatever you have planned, you really don't know what's just around the corner. Are you ready for the unexpected?

👁 Read Ruth 2 v 17–19

ENGAGE YOUR BRAIN

▶ *Boaz was already impressed by Ruth's commitment. Which actions show she's determined and faithful? (v17–18)*

▶ *What makes Naomi so keen to ask questions about her day?*

THINK IT THROUGH

An ephah was a container big enough to climb into — not bad for one day's leftovers! But given what we know about God, should we be surprised when he gives more than the bare minimum?

▶ *How has He gone over the top for you?*

👁 Read Ruth 2 v 19–23

▶ *Naomi's excitement explodes when she finds out who's helping Ruth. What is her view of Boaz's character?*

▶ *How does he show the extra-generosity of God? (v21)*

▶ *What does this offer mean for the two widows?*

Between the ends of chapters 1 and 2 everything has changed. Bitter Naomi can now see a brighter future. It reminds us that with our loving and powerful God there is always hope. If you're in a hole, today could be the day things turn around.

PRAY ABOUT IT

Is there anything good you've given up hoping for? A friend or family member who rejects Jesus? An unfair situation that seems ignored? Bring it back to your Father today, and ask Him for the perseverance that keeps hope alive. (Colossians 1 v 11)

➡ TAKE IT FURTHER

Hold on for some more — page 111.

5 | Comfort vs commitment

How far would you put yourself out for your family? Do someone else's chores? Spend your savings on a gift for them? Marry someone for their benefit???

Read Ruth 3 v 1–9

ENGAGE YOUR BRAIN

▷ *What is Naomi's hope for Ruth? (v1)*

▷ *Why do you think Ruth goes along with the scheme?*

▷ *Although strange to us, Ruth's request was a clear signal to Boaz. What did it mean? (See Ezekiel 16 v 8 for a clue.)*

Put yourself in ancient Israel. You're male and your married brother dies before having kids of his own. The law says you ought to marry his widow — become her "kinsman redeemer". To us, it might sound unfair, but God wanted His people to imitate His amazing covenant love. Commitment was to matter more than convenience.

Read Ruth 3 v 9–18

▷ *What kindness had Ruth already shown? (2 v 11)*

▷ *What was her image among the town's men? (3 v 11)*

▷ *What freedom did she give up for her family?*

Right back at the start of our story, Ruth refused to opt for an easy life in her homeland. At every stage she has been more concerned with loyalty to Naomi than clinging to her rights. And now that she practically has her pick of eligible men, again she chooses what's best for her family.

Jesus surrendered His freedom in praying "not my will, but yours be done." He calls us to the same attitude. The anguish He felt at Gethsemane reminds us that this is far from easy.

GET ON WITH IT

We are called to put commitment before comfort. In what way might following Christ this week mean giving up time, money, popularity?

→ TAKE IT FURTHER

Don't get comfortable, turn to p111.

6 | New-look love

What's the most romantic thing imaginable? A candlelit dinner for two? Serenading your loved one by moonlight? An exotic holiday on paradise island? Get ready for a new-look love.

👁 Read Ruth 4 v 1–6

ENGAGE YOUR BRAIN

▶ *Who witnessed Boaz's meeting?*

▶ *What was the relative's response to the offer of land? (v4)*

▶ *Why did he not want a wife? (v6)*

As we've already seen, Ruth was an attractive proposition! And the relative was not reluctant to buy the land. So why was the idea of marriage a deal breaker? Well, when you sign up as a "kinsman redeemer", your main role is to give the dead man an heir. That means you buy the land, but once you have a son, he gets everything you've paid for. For Ruth's relative, this deal would take a huge chunk away from the inheritance due to his own kids. But Boaz is ready to pay.

👁 Read Ruth 4 v 7–10

▶ *What does the custom of removing a sandal signify?*

▶ *How would you describe the mood of Boaz's summary speech?*

Becoming a kinsman redeemer costs. Yet Boaz seems to celebrate the deal. His speech says: Ruth is mine and I don't care who knows it!

PRAY ABOUT IT

The Bible's model for a husband's love is the self-giving love of Jesus. Not flowers and chocolates, but the commitment of the cross. Is that the kind of marriage you're aiming for? Ask God to develop in you a love that shows something of His passion.

THE BOTTOM LINE

This is love: not that we loved God but that he loved us and sent his son as an atoning sacrifice for sin (1 John 4 v 10).

→ TAKE IT FURTHER

Loving it? Turn to page 111.

7 | The comeback king

The sprinter crosses the finishing line milliseconds before his big rival, and he wins the gold medal. As the world's media surround him, he just smiles and says: "Thanks, Dad!" In his finest hour, he wants someone else to get the glory. Do you?

👁 Read Ruth 4 v 11–15

ENGAGE YOUR BRAIN

▶ Who does the future of this new family depend on? (v11–13)

▶ Why might Ruth's age give new hope to Boaz?

Some people think you get what you deserve. When things go well, we congratulate ourselves for our hard work. But we should really thank God. Right through the Ruth story, He has been at work, invisibly providing for each of our main characters.

👁 Read Ruth 4 v 7–10

▶ What had God provided for childless Naomi?

▶ How will Boaz's arrival change her life?

As kinsman redeemer, Boaz offers new hope to an old lady. His arrival does not just promise food on her table, but the descendants she

dreamed of. It's a small picture of the Great Redeemer, who just loves to turn our despair to joy.

THINK IT THROUGH

▶ How is God working behind the scenes of your own life?

▶ What situation has he redeemed?

▶ In what situation do you need new hope?

PRAY ABOUT IT

Take your thanks for the past and requests for the future to God, who specialises in the glorious comeback.

THE BOTTOM LINE

You turned my wailing into dancing; you removed my sackcloth and clothed me with joy, that my heart may sing to you and not be silent. O Lord my God, I will give you thanks forever. (Psalm 30 v 11–12).

➔ TAKE IT FURTHER

Come back for more on page 111.

8 | History makers

Some people make history. Others end up being part of world-changing events by accident. Either way, just by living for Jesus you'll leave an everlasting legacy. Are you ready to change the world?

👁 Read Ruth 4 v 16–17

ENGAGE YOUR BRAIN

▶ What role and relationship is Naomi given?

As the story ends, we discover a bigger picture. God is using Ruth and Naomi in providing Israel with their greatest king, David. It's a reminder that even the seemingly small details of our humble days can be crucial to His plans.

👁 Read Ruth 4 v 18–22

▶ What country did David's great-grandma, Ruth, come from?

▶ Why might this have surprised some Jews?

▶ Who do you think is the main character in this story?

THINK IT THROUGH

Ultimately, the Bible is one book, with God as its author. That means we can only really understand any part when we see how it fits into the whole. The storyline running throughout is this: Jesus, "Son" of David, and God's rescue through Him.

▶ What have we learned about Jesus through Ruth?

PRAY ABOUT IT

Without knowing it, Ruth has played a key role in God's eternal plan. We can't fully grasp how our actions today might affect future generations. Bring before God your decisions and encounters of the next 24 hours. Pray that He would use you in His mind-blowing purposes.

➡ TAKE IT FURTHER

More big picture stuff on page 111.

What happens next?

Each issue in TRICKY, we tackle those mind-bendingly difficult questions that confuse us all, as well as questions that friends bombard us with to catch us off guard.
This time we ask: is there really life after death?

BYE BYE BODY

None of us can be certain of what will happen in the rest of our lives. We can't be sure how things will turn out or what the future holds. The only thing we can all be certain of is this — one day we will die. It's unavoidable. But then what? Is death the end?

According to the Bible, death *is* the end — for our earthly bodies at least. God created humans out of dust (Genesis 2 v 7) and our bodies will return to dust — dying and decomposing (Ecclesiastes 12 v 6–7). But that doesn't mean death is the end. Far from it. Our spirit (or soul) lives on. The human body is just a temporary home for the human spirit, and it will be replaced by something better (2 Corinthians 5 v 1–5).

ETERNITY NOW

Christians often concentrate so much on this life that we forget there's something far better to come. We should probably stop thinking of life as being in two parts: life on earth and life in heaven. For Christians, eternal life has already begun — those who have trusted in Jesus' death for them possess eternal life. They won't be condemned because they have crossed over from death to life (John 5 v 24).

When believers die, they go to live with Christ in His perfect new world Their imperfect bodies will be turned into glorious new bodies, like Christ's (1 Corinthians 15 v 51–54). So, for Christians, death is actually victory — the start of a new perfect life (Philippians 1 v 21).

JUDGMENT DAY

But this experience is not for everyone. One day, Jesus will return as Judge. All those who trust in Him will be forgiven and go to eternal life, but everyone who rejects Jesus will be sentenced for their sins and go to eternal punishment in hell (Matthew 25 v 31–46). Death is not the end, but where you go depends on Jesus and whether you've trusted Him to save you.

So if there is life after death, what can Christians expect? Well, the Bible tells us that believers will live in God's presence for ever, and they'll be holy (Hebrews 12 v 14). Nothing sinful or imperfect will be there and all the puzzles of this human life will be resolved (1 Corinthians 13 v 9–12). We don't know exactly what it will be like — the Bible only gives us hints — but we do know it will be perfect.

HEAVENLY LIVING

God's word makes it clear that there *is* life after death. This should have a huge impact on our lives.

For those who refuse to live God's way, it means they're heading for eternal punishment. For those who love Jesus, it means they can live life looking forward to an amazing eternity (Hebrews 11 v 16).

Believers should set their standards by those of heaven, rather than those of this sinful world, for they're now citizens of heaven (Philippians 3 v 17–21). They shouldn't care so much about earthly possessions; they're not so important in the context of eternity (Hebrews 10 v 34). They should set their minds on things above, where Christ is, rather than on earthly things (Colossians 3 v 2–4).

Death is not the end, but we need to put ourselves right with God before we reach it. For Christians, their eternal future is safe because of Jesus, so death should hold no fear for them. We should long for eternity with God and let it positively affect the way we live now.

13

Titus

Getting it right

x + y = z. Equations — I'm rubbish at them. But in the Christian life, it's crucial we understand this equation: right belief = right behaviour. Believing right and behaving right are the two halves of the equation. If something is missing from one half or the other, our Christian lives won't add up.

In his letter to Titus, Paul wants to make sure Christians are believing the right things and putting their beliefs into practice. Practising what they preach at home, in work, in society — so that non-Christians will be attracted by the gospel message, as they see it result in changed lives.

Paul is writing to Titus, who was one of his right-hand men. Titus travelled around with Paul through places like Asia Minor and Greece as Paul preached about Jesus and set up churches (groups of Christians) in various places he visited.

On their travels, Paul and Titus went to the Greek island of Crete, though not for the snorkeling. They went to preach the gospel, and their visit to Crete was a great success — many of the islanders becoming Christians. Paul left Crete, but Titus stayed.

Paul wants Titus to make sure the Christians on Crete get the equation right: believe the right things and live out their beliefs in the real world, so that other people will want to become Christians.

As we read Titus, we'll see it's bang up to date. Nothing is more of a turn-off in a Christian than hypocrisy. And nothing is more appealing in a Christian than to see him or her getting the equation right. Right belief = right behaviour.

9 ⫶ Hi, Titus!

How would you begin a letter or email to a friend? "Hi Jane, how's things?" Well, Paul's letter to Titus doesn't start off quite so simply. Actually, it's completely fact-packed.

👁 Read Titus 1 v 1

ENGAGE YOUR BRAIN
▷ What do we learn about Paul?

▷ Why does he spread the message of Jesus?

Paul describes himself as an apostle — someone sent to share the truth about Jesus' death and resurrection. He serves God by helping to build up the faith of God's chosen people ("the elect", Christians). He wants people to understand the truth so they live the kind of lifestyle God wants. Notice how the equation appears in this very first verse: right belief = right behaviour.

👁 Read verses 2–3
▷ What does faith in Jesus rest on? (v2)

▷ What has God promised to believers? (v2)

▷ And why can we trust Him? (v2)

👁 Read verse 4
▷ What does Paul call Titus?

▷ What makes them so close?

At the heart of this letter is Jesus. God kept His promise and sent Jesus to rescue people and give them eternal life. If we know this great truth, then we should want to live in a way that pleases God. Just as Paul and Titus did.

THINK IT OVER
▷ What would you say to a friend who says they believe the gospel but doesn't live a godly lifestyle?

PRAY ABOUT IT
Ask God to help you believe His great promises and live in a way that shows you do.

THE BOTTOM LINE
Right belief = right behaviour.

→ TAKE IT FURTHER
Right. Turn to page 112. Right now.

10 | Lead by example

What qualities do you think a church leader should have?
1.   2.
3.   4.
Let's see if Paul agrees.

👁 Read Titus 1 v 5-7

ENGAGE YOUR BRAIN

▶ *What was Titus' job? (v5)*

▶ *What should a church leader's family life be like? (v6)*

▶ *What should a leader NOT be like? (v7)*

A church is a family of believers. So a church leader should have a good family life at home too. If one of your parents is a church leader, remember that how you live affects how others view them. A church leader (or "elder" or "overseer") should set a good example, not a bad one (v7).

👁 Read verses 8–9

▶ *In your own words, describe what a church leader should be like (v8)*

▶ *What must he do? (v9)*

▶ *What two things will this enable him to do?*

Good leaders must practise what they preach. If they do that and stick to God's word, they'll encourage believers to grow and be able to stand up to opposition.

PRAY ABOUT IT

Pray for Christian leaders you know. Thank God for them. Pray that they will live up to this tough job description and continue to teach God's word and live by it.

THE BOTTOM LINE

Christian leaders must lead by example.

➡ TAKE IT FURTHER

Follow the leader to page 112.

11 Dishonest deceivers

Remember the equation? Right belief = right behaviour. Well, the opposite is true. Wrong belief = wrong behaviour. There were people in the church in Crete who were teaching rubbish and leading Christians astray.

👁 Read Titus 1 v 10–16

ENGAGE YOUR BRAIN

▶ *How does Paul describe these troublemakers? (v10)*

▶ *What were they doing? (v11)*

▶ *What should Titus do about it? (v11, v13–14)*

The "circumcision group" told Christians they must keep Jewish rules like getting circumcised and not eating pork etc. Paul called these rules "Jewish myths" (v14). They were causing great damage, ripping families apart and gaining from it (v11). So Paul told Titus to take a hardline approach, silencing such teaching and making sure no believers fell for it.

Yesterday we heard that it's essential for Christian leaders to "hold firmly to the trustworthy message as it has been taught" (v9). This was the message about Christ, taught by Paul and the apostles. We have their teaching in the New Testament.

THINK IT OVER

▶ *So how can we spot false teachers today?*

▶ *How will their beliefs and behaviour give them away? (v15–16)*

If you're unsure about any teaching you hear, check it with the Bible. Is it in line with what God's word says? And ask a mature Christian you respect about it too.

PRAY ABOUT IT

Pray for Christian leaders you know that they'll have the courage to stand up against those who teach wrong things. Pray that you'll know your Bible better so you won't be taken in by such teaching.

→ TAKE IT FURTHER

More about "Jewish myths" on p112.

12 | Equal to the task

Think of older Christians you know. How can you learn from them? And how is their example not always a good one?

👁 Read Titus 2 v 1–2

ENGAGE YOUR BRAIN

▶ *How should Titus teach?*

▶ *What should older Christian guys be like?*

Titus should teach stuff that's in line with "sound doctrine". Sound here means "healthy". Titus is to teach the Christians in Crete to live a healthy Christian lifestyle. For Christian men, that means living lives that set a good example to younger men — being self-controlled, full of faith and love, and keeping going as Christians.

👁 Read verses 3–5

▶ *How should older Christian women live? (v3)*

▶ *What about younger women? (v4–5)*

Young Christian women should look up to more mature women and learn from them. They should not get addicted to booze and shouldn't spread false rumours about people. Self-control and purity are the order of the day.

If you're married, you should love your husband and kids, remembering that the husband is the head of the family. Paul isn't saying Christian women should be timid or stay at home and not have a job. He's saying that if you have a husband and kids; love them, don't neglect them. The key thing here is that Christians should act in a way that doesn't reflect badly on God and His word.

GET ON WITH IT

▶ *Which older Christians can you spend more time with?*

▶ *What can you learn from them?*

▶ *Have these verses reminded you of anything you need to sort out?*

→ TAKE IT FURTHER

More on these issues on page 112.

13 ¦ Life lessons

Yesterday we read Paul's advice to young Christian women. Today he turns his attention to young Christian men. And slaves. But there are valuable lessons here for all of us.

👁 Read Titus 2 v 6–8

ENGAGE YOUR BRAIN

▷ *What does it mean to be self-controlled?*

▷ *Specifically, how do you need to show more self-control?*

▷ *Why must Titus watch what he preaches and the way he lives? (v7–8)*

👁 Read verse 9–10

▷ *What will be the result if Christians keep Paul's principles and work hard? (v10)*

In this chapter, Paul keeps repeating the fact that the way we act will affect non-believers. Whatever they say about us, non-Christians always keep an eye on Christians to see if they practise what they preach.

If we lead a life of love, faith and self-control then it reflects well on the gospel. If we show no self-control and have messed up relationships at home, work or church, then the gospel will seem unattractive.

Think how you can improve your act as a Christian at home, at college/ school, when you're at a party, at work... so that non-Christians are attracted to Jesus. God has rescued us for heaven and has restored our broken relationship with Him. So let's live for Him.

PRAY ABOUT IT

Pray that you and your Christian friends would live genuine Christ-honouring lives, so that your unbelieving friends will find the message about Jesus attractive and want to become Christians too.

THE BOTTOM LINE

Live for God. You're being watched.

➡ TAKE IT FURTHER

More life lessons on page 113.

14 | Heart of the message

**This section is the heart of this great letter.
Here, Paul gives us another equation:
healthy teaching = healthy lifestyle.**

👁 Read Titus 2 v 11–15

ENGAGE YOUR BRAIN

▷ *Who or what is Paul talking about in v11?*

▷ *What does Jesus' death and resurrection teach us to say "no" to? (v12)*

▷ *What should we replace these things with? (v12)*

The "grace of God" is Paul's shorthand for everything the Lord Jesus has done for us. Coming into this world to show us what God is like; dying to free us from God's punishment, which our rebellion deserves; rising from the dead to give us the hope of eternal life.

▷ *What's the great hope that Christians wait for? (v13)*

▷ *Why did Jesus die on the cross? (v14)*

This is what Christianity is all about. Jesus gave Himself for us — dying, to buy us back from sin, making us His own people and purifying us. We should respond by doing "what is good" as we wait for Him to return in glory.

GET ON WITH IT

We should look back to what Jesus did for us on the cross and look forward to the glorious future when He returns.

▷ *How will those two events affect the way you live now?*

PRAY ABOUT IT

Please pray that you, us and every Christian will realise how much we owe the Lord Jesus and long to live to please Him.

THE BOTTOM LINE

We owe everything to Jesus.

→ TAKE IT FURTHER

A little more heart on page 113.

15 Get on with it!

This great letter keeps reminding us that if we trust in Jesus, then we should live in a way that shows it and attracts others. So how can we actually do that?

👁 Read Titus 3 v 1–2

This is not just theory — if you're serious about Jesus, then it's time to start living in a way that shows it. Let's get practical. Make sure you write down your answers.

GET ON WITH IT

▶ Who should we be obedient to? (v1)

▶ How should this change the way you treat...
teachers/bosses?

parents?

the law?

Christian leaders?

▶ So what will you do about it?

▶ What should you be prepared for? (v1)

▶ What "good" do you fail to do?

▶ Who do you badmouth?

▶ Who do you need to make peace with?

▶ How can you make sure you don't lose it next time someone teases you?

▶ How can you be more considerate with the people you spend most time with?

▶ How will you be more humble and less full of yourself?

PRAY ABOUT IT

Now read through your answers and talk to God about them, one by one. Ask Him to help you make the changes you need to.

THE BOTTOM LINE

Being a Christian means living with Christ at the centre of your life.

→ TAKE IT FURTHER

More about authority on page 113.

16 | Bath time

Before becoming Christians, we all believed wrongly and lived wrongly. What difference does becoming a Christian make? What difference has it made in your life?

👁 Read Titus 3 v 3

ENGAGE YOUR BRAIN

▷ What's life like before people turn to Christ?

▷ What rules their lives?

▷ How were/are you like this?

👁 Read verses 4–6

▷ Who gets the credit for you becoming a Christian?

▷ Did you deserve to be saved? (v5)

▷ How were you saved? (v5–6)

▷ What do these verses tell us about God's character?

👁 Read verses 7–8

▷ What is the future for believers? (v7)

▷ If we believe all these things, what should be the result? (v8)

Before we became Christians, our lives were a mess. We didn't deserve anything from God yet He mercifully rescued us from our sinful lives. He sent Jesus to die in our place so that our lives could be washed clean and renewed by the Holy Spirit. Christians are "justified" (v7) — put right with God, forgiven, accepted by Him. So they should be careful to devote themselves to doing what is good (v8).

GET ON WITH IT

▷ Have you trusted in God yet?

▷ If so, are you still trusting Him?

▷ Are you being careful? And devoted?

▷ What can you do that's good for others?

PRAY ABOUT IT

Thank God for giving you a bath. Tell God all the credit goes to Him for saving you. And ask Him to help you get the equation right. Right belief = right behaviour.

→ TAKE IT FURTHER

From bath time to birth time: p113.

17 | Argu-mental

What do you tend to have arguments about? What topics get you fired up? What issues cause divisions between your friends? What about in your church / youth group?

👁 Read Titus 3 v 9

ENGAGE YOUR BRAIN

▶ *What kinds of arguments should Christians avoid?*

▶ *Why?*

This doesn't mean we should never have discussions and disagreements about Christian stuff. After all, Jesus caused plenty of controversy and debate. It's healthy to get excited about the Bible and moral issues.

Paul says avoid "foolish" controversies — stuff that's pointless and causes divisions. If you're ever in the middle of a heated debate, think to yourself: is this important? If you're defending the gospel, go for it! If you're getting aggressive about whether hamsters go to heaven, maybe you could let it drop.

👁 Read verses 10–11

▶ *How should someone who causes splits be treated at first?*

▶ *What if they continue to cause trouble?*

If someone is causing splits between Christians, get a leader to talk with them. If they continue to cause problems, then we should have nothing to do with them.

THINK IT OVER

▶ *What pointless arguments do you get involved in?*

▶ *What do you say or do that might cause division?*

PRAY ABOUT IT

Ask God for unity in your church / youth group. Ask Him for help in deciding which discussions are worth having and which ones are a waste of time.

THE BOTTOM LINE

Avoid foolish controversies

➔ TAKE IT FURTHER

More arguing on page 114.

18 Fond farewell

They think it's all over. But it isn't. Yet. Paul finishes off his letter with some instructions for Titus and a final word of encouragement.

👁 Read Titus 3 v 12–13

Paul is going to send Artemas and his (possibly shorter) colleague Tychicus to Crete. They will replace Titus, who's needed in Nicopolis, a city in mainland Greece.

ENGAGE YOUR BRAIN

▷ How does Paul sending Artemas and Tychicus show his concern for the new Christians on Crete?

▷ And how should Titus treat Zenas and Apollos?

👁 Read verses 14–15

▷ What does Paul say fellow believers should be devoted to?

▷ Why?

Paul's equation comes back one last time. Right belief = right behaviour. It's one thing to believe the truth about Jesus, but we've got to live it too. That means devoting our lives to serving Him and doing what is good. So that our lives aren't unproductive.

PRAY ABOUT IT

Thank God for what you've learned from Titus, for the equation, for God's love for you, and for Jesus who gave Himself for you.

Pray that God would help you grow in knowledge and understanding of the Bible, so you'll know the difference between sick and healthy teaching.

Pray that you'll make God's saving message attractive to non-Christians you know and meet.

→ TAKE IT FURTHER

One last visit to Titus on page 114.

19 | Judge dread

Before we jump into 1 Samuel, it's time for a psalm break. Psalm 82 is a dark and tricky one, but stick with it and you'll learn something about our great God.

👁 Read Psalm 82 v 1–5

ENGAGE YOUR BRAIN

▶ What's the scene? (v1)

▶ What is God's role? (v1)

▶ What annoys Him? (v2)

▶ What had people been failing to do? (v3–4)

▶ What does this reveal about them? v5)

The tricky bit in this psalm is identifying who the "gods" are (v1, v6). Are they: a) those who were judges among God's people; b) spiritual powers; c) something else? We vote for a) but won't get upset if you disagree.

God looked for His people to live His way, as they should. But they were failing to look after those who were weak, poor or downtrodden.

👁 Read verses 6–8

▶ What will happen to rulers who fail to rule fairly? (v7)

▶ What does the psalm writer ask God to do? (v8)

▶ What reason does he give?

One day, God will summon the whole earth before Him. He'll take charge of that court and pass judgment. Those who've failed to serve Him or treat people rightly will be punished. It's a sobering thought. And a direct challenge for God's people now to get living God's way.

PRAY ABOUT IT

Thank God that He's in charge and He's perfectly fair. Pray that you will "defend the cause of the weak and fatherless" and "maintain the rights of the poor and oppressed".

➔ TAKE IT FURTHER

A tiny bit more on page 114.

Abortion

One minute it's a heated debate at school, the next it's something incredibly painful a friend is dealing with. In the UK alone, close to 200,000 abortions were performed in 2009. However much we might not want to think about it, it's an issue that isn't going away. So what does the Bible have to say on the subject?

Firstly, human life is valuable. We are made in the image of God (Genesis 1 v 26–27). He's the one who gives life — it's a precious gift and taking it is against God's law (Exodus 20 v 13). But when does human life begin? Logically it has to be either at conception or birth, rather than a random number of weeks into the foetus' development. The Bible tells us that God "knit me together in my mother's womb" (Psalm 139 v 13). John the Baptist leaped for joy in his mother's womb when she met Mary the mother of Jesus (Luke 1 v 41). David talks of being a sinner even when his mother conceived him (Psalm 51 v 5). Clearly, human life begins at conception.

One of the arguments you may have heard is that a women has the right to choose what happens to her own body, and that sounds pretty reasonable. But the fact of the matter is that an unborn baby is an entirely separate genetic being; not merely part of his or her mother's body. Yes, he or she depends totally on his or her mother for survival, but in a way so does a newborn baby. If we stopped feeding and keeping a newborn baby warm or safe, he or she would soon die, and that, rightly, would be classed as murder.

But what about cases where the mother's life is in danger or the baby is severely disabled and unlikely to survive? Or what about cases of rape or incest — surely we can't expect people to decide against abortion in those circumstances? Staggeringly, the number of abortions which fall into this category every year is less than 2%. Even minor disabilities or deformities such as a cleft lip, which can be corrected by a simple operation, can be used as reasons to abort an "imperfect" baby.

In genuinely difficult circumstances, we must be careful to avoid being

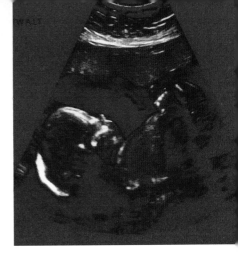

judgmental and harsh — unless we have been there we cannot know the trauma and pain faced by a survivor of rape or incest or someone faced with the knowledge their baby is severely disabled. But there have been many instances of people in those situations who have given their baby a chance of life and who, despite the pain, have known God's blessing and presence with them. Check out your local Christian bookshop for many real-life examples.

Christians are at the forefront of the anti-abortion or "right to life" campaign. There are regular opportunities to speak out on this issue as governments debate lowering the time limits on abortion, as the morning after pill (which provides an early chemical abortion) becomes more widely available, or as abortion providers are increasingly allowed to advertise in the media. If this is something you feel you would like to be involved with, there are plenty of organisations to help you campaign on this issue — see below. Christians must be prepared to put their time and money where their mouth is and offer support mums in non-ideal circumstances.

But maybe, all this is making you feel terribly guilty. Maybe you or a friend made a mistake; thought abortion was the only way out or were pressured into it. Maybe your girlfriend decided to have an abortion and you didn't speak out but didn't want it to happen. Maybe you feel as if God can never forgive you and you'll be living with the pain for the rest of your life. Take heart. God knows our darkest secrets and can forgive our most horrible sins.

Three of the writers of the Bible committed murder — Moses, David and Saul/Paul. God showed His grace and mercy to them and they lived as His forgiven and hugely loved children. As Jesus was being crucified He prayed: "Father, forgive them" for His executioners (Luke 23 v 34). Our God is a God of incredible grace and mercy and "if anyone is in Christ that person is a new creation. The old has gone, the new is here!" (2 Corinthians 5 v 17).

Useful links:
Campaigning: www.spuc.org.uk
Counselling: www.careconfidential.com

1 Samuel

Long live the king!

"The king is dead! Long live the king!" Ever heard that line in a movie? One monarch dies, but the next one immediately takes his place. Sounds all very neat and tidy. The handover between Saul and his successor was far messier than that.

These next 15 chapters of 1 Samuel are full of intrigue, attempted murder, battles, narrow escapes, sorcery, kidnapping and tragedy. Not to mention victories, friendship, love, dramatic rescues and the incredible faithfulness of God to His promises.

Israel's first king, Saul, has turned out to be a bit of a disaster; concerned more for his own honour than obeying God's commands. But God has someone better in mind (actually, He has someone even better than that ultimately in mind!). Enter David. Shepherd boy, musician, giant-killer and all round good guy. Well, not quite. He needs to learn to put God

first and obey Him completely as we'll see, but David's heart is in the right place.

Of course the best thing about David is that he has the honour of being Jesus' great-great-great-great (you get the picture) grandfather. And as we see David learning what it takes to be a king, we get glimpses of what God's perfect King, Jesus, will be like.

So read on and thank God that Christians can say "Long live the King!" knowing that Jesus reigns forever.

A new king

The whole king experiment has not gone well so far. Saul has failed to obey God and God has rejected him. But the story doesn't finish there. God has plans for a new king.

👁 Read 1 Samuel 16 v 1–13

ENGAGE YOUR BRAIN

▶ *What does God want Samuel to do? (v1)*

▶ *Why might this be dangerous? (v2)*

▶ *Who is Samuel reminded is in charge? (v3)*

▶ *Who does Samuel think God has chosen? (v6)*

▶ *Why? (v7a)*

▶ *What does God look for? (v7b)*

▶ *What is surprising about God's choice as the next king? (v11)*

▶ *What marks David out as God's chosen king? (v13)*

PRAY ABOUT IT

Are you tempted to judge people on their outward appearance? Ask God to help you look at their hearts. Do you know someone who is popular but has no time for Jesus, or someone who is deeply uncool but lives for God? Ask God to change the way you think about and value these people.

David may seem an unlikely choice, but it's all part of God's master plan. Check out Matthew 1 v 6 all the way to v16. David will be a great king but his descendant will be the greatest King.

THE BOTTOM LINE
God chooses His king.

→ TAKE IT FURTHER
More kingly stuff on page 114.

21 Saul gone wrong

Sometimes when you're watching a film, you know something the other characters don't. There's a certain dramatic irony here as Saul becomes pals with the guy who's going to replace him...

Read 1 Samuel 16 v 14–23

▷ *What is Saul's problem? (v14)*

Saul had gone against God and now we see God abandoning him, and worse, going against Saul. This is still true today for people who reject God. The consequences both now and in eternity are not just the absence of God from your life but His anger against you. Scary stuff.

PRAY ABOUT IT

Pray for those you know who are currently rejecting Jesus. Thank God that He has given them time and opportunity to repent, and pray that they'd do so.

▷ *What solution do Saul's advisors suggest? (v16)*

▷ *And who do they find to supply the music therapy? (v19)*

▷ *Are things looking positive for David and Saul? (v21–23)*

▷ *Do you think it will last?*

GET ON WITH IT

If you are currently going against God; stop. Say sorry and ask for His forgiveness.

THE BOTTOM LINE

You don't want God as your enemy.

→ TAKE IT FURTHER

A little more on page 114.

22 | Gigantic battle

A famous story today but before we get into "who are the Goliaths in your life?" and "even the smallest person can make a difference", let's see what this story really teaches us!

👁 Read 1 Samuel 17 v 1–37

ENGAGE YOUR BRAIN

▷ Who is threatening the Israelites? (v1–3)

▷ What does Goliath propose as a way of settling the war's outcome? (v8–9)

▷ Would you be up for fighting him? (see v4–7)

▷ How do Saul and the Israelites react? (v11)

▷ How long does this state of affairs go on? (v16)

▷ Again, which of Jesse's sons are likely heroes? (v13–14)

▷ What are David's jobs? (v15, v17–18)

A shepherd come pizza delivery boy. Yet again, David is not looking a very likely hero. But remember that God looks at the heart, not the outward appearance.

▷ What is in Goliath's heart? (v10, v26)

▷ What about Saul and the Israelites? (v11, v24, v32)

▷ What about David? Is Eliab's accusation correct? (v28, v26, v36–37)

PRAY ABOUT IT

When you face people who are mocking or aggressive towards our faith and our God, are you scared and intimidated? Ask God to help you be concerned for His glory like David. Ask Him to help you make a stand for Him.

THE BOTTOM LINE

In your heart set apart Christ as Lord (1 Peter 3 v 15).

→ TAKE IT FURTHER

Time for a substitution on page 114.

23 | Stone dead

A massive warrior against a young lad. A sword, spear and javelin versus a handful of small stones. It looks like a very unequal match. And so it is, but not in the way you might think.

👁 Read 1 Samuel 17 v 38–47

▶ *What is the key thing to remember in this battle? (v37)*

▶ *How do we know that David is trusting in the Lord alone? (v38–40)*

▶ *What point does David make? (v47)*

▶ *Who and what is Goliath trusting in? (v43–45)*

It's a very unequal match. Some man-made false gods and a load of man-made armour versus the living God. Goliath has no chance!

👁 Read verses 48–58

▶ *What happens? (v48–50)*

▶ *What is the outcome for the Israelites and Philistines? (v51–53)*

▶ *What will be the long-term outcome? (v46)*

Just as with the rescue from Egypt, the end goal of God's powerful saving acts is that the whole world should know Him.

SHARE IT

God has acted in your life for His glory, so that people around you might come to know Him. Have you ever realised that before? Can you tell someone today / this week how God rescued you from death and sin by His Son dying in your place? Be brave — the Lord is with you!

THE BOTTOM LINE

The whole world will know there is a God.

→ TAKE IT FURTHER

More giant-killing on page 114.

24 | From nice to nasty

After the triumph over the Philistines,
things are looking good for David.
But not for long...

Read 1 Samuel 18 v 1–16

ENGAGE YOUR BRAIN

▶ How does Saul's son treat David?
(v1-4)

▶ What does this show he
recognises about David? (v4)

▶ How does Saul treat David? (v5)

▶ How do the people react to
David? (v5–7, v16)

▶ What effect does this have on
Saul? (v9)

▶ What happens next? (v10–11)

Saul is jealous of David and God
sends an evil spirit on him. Saul
chooses to act on his jealousy but it's
also within God's control. Confusing?
Yep, but it's happened before
(Pharaoh in Exodus 7 v 13).

TALK IT OVER

We often struggle with the idea that
people make choices but God is also
in control. The Bible teaches that we
are responsible for our actions and
that God is in charge. Chat and
pray about these things with an
older Christian.

▶ How does Saul seek to get rid of
David (v13)?

▶ Does it work?

▶ Why? What phrase is repeated
(v12, v14)?

PRAY ABOUT IT

However much opposition you face,
whatever is in store, good or bad; if
you belong to Jesus, you are on the
winning side. God promises to be
with you (Matthew 28 v 20). Thank
Him now.

THE BOTTOM LINE

God is in control.

→ TAKE IT FURTHER

Big Bible bits on page 115.

33

25 | Family misfortune

Saul is still trying sneaky ways to get rid of David, but he ends up with him as his son-in-law! You can't outmanoeuvre God...

👁 Read 1 Samuel 18 v 17–30

ENGAGE YOUR BRAIN

▷ *What's the carrot Saul offers David at first? (v17)*

▷ *What is he hoping will happen?*

▷ *How does David feel about becoming part of Saul's family (v18)?*

You might expect David to become quite arrogant as a result of all the praise and success he's been getting, but he stays humble. His heart still pleases God.

▷ *What is Saul's next tactic? (v20–25)*

Nice wedding present? Think I'd prefer a toaster. Still, Saul reckons this is an impossible task which will hopefully finish David off. Guess again!

▷ *Why does David succeed? (v28)*

▷ *What effect does this have on Saul? (v29)*

Verse 29 is really tragic. The king of Israel is afraid of David and becomes his enemy. Why? Because the Lord is with him. It shows just how far Saul has fallen. It seems hard to understand that someone would be hostile to someone else just because God is with them, but the Bible is full of examples of this. See Jesus for the ultimate example.

▷ *How did Jesus react? (Luke 23 v 32–34)*

PRAY ABOUT IT

Use Matthew 5 v 43–45 to kickstart your prayers today.

THE BOTTOM LINE

You can't outmanoeuvre God.

→ TAKE IT FURTHER

Check out page 115.

26 | Friends and enemies

Saul's murderous plans show no sign of stopping. Fortunately David has a good friend in Jonathan; a friend God has provided.

👁 Read 1 Samuel 19 v 1–24

ENGAGE YOUR BRAIN

▶ *What is Saul's plan (v1)?*
▶ *How does Jonathan persuade him differently? (v2–5)*
▶ *Does Saul listen? (v6)*
▶ *How long does that last? (v8–10)*
▶ *Who else helps David? (v11–17)*
▶ *And who else? (v18)*
▶ *Who is behind all of these people helping David?*

Jonathan and Michal were Saul's own children. Samuel was his official prophet. No wonder Saul felt that everyone was against him. But who was behind it all? God. Remember God had rejected Saul for turning away from Him (1 Samuel 15 v 26).

David was God's chosen king and yet he still faced persecution. Jesus had to deal with His family thinking He was crazy (Mark 3 v 21). By following God's chosen king, Jonathan and Michal risked their father's disapproval and hostility.

TALK IT OVER

Read Matthew 10 v 34–39 and Mark 10 v 28–30 with a Christian friend. Do you face disapproval or even outright hostility from your family or friends because you follow Jesus? Take heart from these verses and pray about it together.

PRAY ABOUT IT

Many Christians in countries hostile to Christianity face rejection by their families and even death for choosing to follow Jesus Christ. Pray for them now; for strength, for courage, for God to help them to stand firm and to rejoice in His presence with them and for His gift of eternal life.

→ TAKE IT FURTHER

More friendly words on page 115.

27 | Splitting heirs

Who do you trust? Who is going to keep their promises? Things start getting more and more tangled in Saul's disintegrating reign as king.

Read 1 Samuel 20 v 1–42

ENGAGE YOUR BRAIN

▶ *What is David trying to discover? (v1)*

▶ *What is his friend's reaction? (v2)*

▶ *Does David believe him? (v3)*

▶ *What plan do they hatch? (v4–23)*

▶ *Is Saul still trying to kill David? (v30–34)*

▶ *Who are David and Jonathan relying on? (v3, v12, v13, v14, v16, v21, v23, v42)*

David and Jonathan both recognise God's power and faithful love. Jonathan even prays that God would be with David as He was once with Saul (v14). They base their friendship on the way God acts — wanting to be faithful as He is.

▶ *How is Jonathan's behaviour (v42) different to Saul's (v31)?*

PRAY ABOUT IT

God promises to make us, as Christians, more and more like His Son. Ask Him now to help you to be faithful in keeping promises and to show unfailing kindness and love to people as Jesus does.

THE BOTTOM LINE

God's faithful love lasts for ever.

→ TAKE IT FURTHER

Promising stuff on page 115.

28 ¦ Going crazy ¦

David's on the run and there's a lot of ducking and diving to stay safe in this chapter. Thing is, God's still perfectly in control...

👁 **Read 1 Samuel 21 v 1–9**

ENGAGE YOUR BRAIN

▷ *What does David need from Ahimelech? (v3)*

▷ *Is David being strictly truthful? (v2, v5)*

▷ *What else is he after? (v8)*

▷ *What's his excuse for his lack of weapons? (v8)*

▷ *What does he end up with? (v9)*

Despite his rather poor excuses, David ends up with what he desperately needs — food and protection. But where does he head with Goliath's old sword? Only Goliath's home town!

👁 **Read verses 10–15**

▷ *Is it surprising he was recognised? (v11)*

▷ *What is David's tactic to stay safe this time? (v13)*

▷ *Does it work?*

The Bible doesn't tell us whether David did the right thing or not and he certainly deceives various people in this chapter. But look how desperate things are — he's on the run and in danger of losing his life.

PRAY ABOUT IT

Do you ever feel that you are running round in a panic? Stop for a minute and remember that God is in control. Talk to Him about the things that stress you out. Remember that if you have put your trust in Jesus: your past is dealt with, He is with you in the present and your future is secure.

THE BOTTOM LINE
God is with us.

➔ **TAKE IT FURTHER**
Run along to page 115.

29 | Outlaw and disorder

David gets himself a bunch of outlaws. It's not quite Robin Hood, but the distressed, the debtors and the discontented make up a formidable bunch. This next chapter makes for unpleasant reading.

Read 1 Samuel 22 v 1–23

ENGAGE YOUR BRAIN

▶ *Who follows David into hiding? (v1–2)*

▶ *What is David worried about? (v3–4)*

▶ *What does God tell David to do? (v5)*

▶ *Does this seem safe?*

▶ *Does David obey?*

▶ *How would you describe Saul's frame of mind? (v7–8)*

▶ *How about his behaviour? (v17–19)*

Doeg is a nasty piece of work, and he'll get his comeuppance eventually, but not before a lot of innocent people — even children and babies — are massacred.

▶ *How does David respond to the news of the massacre? (v22)*

How different to Saul! David takes responsibility even though it's not really his fault and offers protection to Abiathar. Saul does anything he can to avoid facing up to the fact that God has deserted him, and murderously takes it out on the innocent.

PRAY ABOUT IT

Some horrible things happen in our fallen world. Thank God that one day He will return as Judge and justice will be done. But also thank God that He doesn't want anyone to perish and that He poured out His terrible anger and judgment on Jesus so that we could be forgiven.

TAKE IT FURTHER

Time for another psalm on page 116.

30 | King of everything

Here's a psalm that keeps us hanging on right to its last verse. It's only then that we grasp just what the writer wants and why that's so crucial. It opens with God's people in trouble...

👁 Read Psalm 83 v 1–8

ENGAGE YOUR BRAIN

▶ What was the crisis? (v3–4)

▶ Who were they actually fighting? (v5)

▶ What did the writer want from God? (v1)

Israel was effectively surrounded on all sides (v6–7), with even the bullying world superpower Assyria involved (v8). And God seemed to be distant, silent, uninvolved. Time to panic!

👁 Read verses 9–18

▶ What did the writer remember God had done in the past? (v9–12)

▶ What did he want God to do now? (v13–15)

▶ With what outcome? (v16–17)

▶ What did he most want to happen? (v18)

God over all. The world's sole Ruler. And He's "the Lord" — the one who committed Himself to His people. Incredible. The writer wanted to see the world that opposed God and His people brought to realise exactly who God is.

PRAY ABOUT IT

Pray for people you know who are against God and His people. Pray that they'd realise who God is — the King over everything.

→ TAKE IT FURTHER

Background battles on page 116.

Amazing grace

In *Essential*, we take time out to explore key truths about God, the Bible and Christianity. This issue, we ask the question: what's this grace thing all about?

AMAZING GRACE

"I live a good life." "I've never murdered anyone." "I go to church." "Yeah – I plan to go to heaven."

Ever heard anyone say that? Ever thought it? Lots of us have! Human beings have an independent streak. We like to think that we can impress God and persuade Him that we are good enough to be accepted by Him. We're aware there are lots of times we mess up too but the bottom line is that many of us would like to earn God's love and acceptance all by ourselves.

However, God knows differently. He knows that no matter how hard we try we can never reach His standards. We are sinners — rebels whose nature is to ignore God and His ways — and we deserve punishment (Romans 3 v 10–12). And He knows there's no way we can wriggle out

of that punishment. Helping little old ladies and excelling in our studies are good things to do but they can never make up for our sinfulness. We can't do good works and expect God to say: "Oh, ok, I'll forget about all your sin" (Titus 3 v 5).

So is there any hope of us reaching eternal life? Well, there is!

SOVEREIGN GRACE

God is passionate about grace. In fact grace is part of God's character (1 Peter 5 v 10). God loves to shower good things on people who deserve punishment. It is His nature to love the unlovely, forgive the guilty and rescue the lost. That's grace and it's amazing.

Right from the start of the Bible we see grace in action. God continued to care for Adam and Eve, by giving them clothes and hope, even after

they disobeyed Him (Genesis 3). In the New Testament, we see grace reach its climax. When Jesus came to earth, it was to bring God's grace to the whole world (John 1 v 17).

SAVING GRACE

When Jesus died on the cross and rose again to take the punishment we deserve, that was grace in action. That was God's way of giving people who deserve punishment the best present — the gift of forgiveness and a new relationship with Him (Ephesians 2 v 5).

When God calls us to follow Him, that's grace (Galatians 1 v 15). When we say sorry to God and respond to Him in faith, that's God's grace helping us to do something great that we could never do by ourselves (2 Timothy 2 v 25; Ephesians 2 v 8–9). Joining God's family has nothing to do with how good we are — it's all about God's grace swinging into action.

GIFTS OF GRACE

Staying in God's family forever is all about grace too. We don't have to do things to persuade God to keep on loving us.

He gives all believers gifts of grace to equip them to serve Him and other people (Romans 12 v 6). When we pray for our non-Christian friends and tell other people about Jesus, God's grace is at work enabling others to respond to His offer of forgiveness (Acts 14 v 26). When we reflect on the wonder of grace, we are gradually changed to become the people that God wants us to be (Titus 2 v 11–12). And when we mess up, God's grace means He is willing to keep on forgiving us, no matter how many times we get things wrong (Matthew 18 v 21–35).

Grace lies at the heart of our salvation and our Christian life. So much so that Paul calls the message of Christianity, the "gospel of grace" (Acts 20 v 24). Why not thank God for His grace now and ask Him to help you trust that His grace is sufficient for all your needs? (2 Corinthians 12 v 9)

Isaiah

God's perfect city

We began our look at the huge book of Isaiah last issue. The story so far: Isaiah has been passing on a vision from God about Jerusalem and Judah (God's people) — how they'd be punished for turning away from Him. But also God's plans for a new, perfect Jerusalem.

Chapters 1–5: Rebellion
God's people disobey Him and are heading for His punishment. But there are signs that God hasn't given up on them yet.

Chapters 6–12: Perfect King
God will raise up a ruler from King David's family who will reign forever.

Chapters 13–27: A coming day
God rules nations, and He shows it in acts of judgment that point us ahead to God's world-shaking final day.

Chapters 28–39:Undeserved rescue
God will punish His own people too,

but amazingly, will show them mercy.

And now for chapters 40–66, the second part of Isaiah's vision. Here, Isaiah's book builds up to a vision of a new Jerusalem — a transformed city filled with people who know God's forgiveness and share His presence. It's a great prospect.

At the centre of God's plans for Jerusalem is a King who'd achieve God's purposes by acting as God's servant and then as a conquering hero.

Come and look through God's plans for this perfect city, the new Jerusalem, that awaits those who trust God and His King.

31 | God's highway

The first few verses of chapter 40 set the tone for the second half of Isaiah. The first half had loads about God's judgment on those who rebelled against Him. But it seems the future is much brighter for God's people.

👁 Read Isaiah 40 v 1–2

ENGAGE YOUR BRAIN

▶ *After the terrifying visions of judgment, what was now the message for God's people? (v1)*

▶ *What's the encouraging news of v2?*

Incredible. Despite all their sin and rebellion, they were still God's people. Eventually they would be freed and forgiven. And their sin problem would be settled in a far greater way than they'd ever imagined.

👁 Read verses 3–5

▶ *Who did they need to get ready for? (v3)*

▶ *What will be revealed? (v5)*

▶ *Who will see this?*

The Lord is about to visit His people, so preparations must be made. No one will fail to notice when He arrives and God's glory is revealed. The first few verses of Isaiah 40 point us to King Jesus, who would pay for the sins of His people and lead them home.

THINK IT OVER

▶ *Have you trusted in Jesus to forgive your sins?*

▶ *Are you ready for His return?*

▶ *Are you looking forward to Him taking you "home" to His city?*

PRAY ABOUT IT

Put today's verses into your own words to express your thanks and excitement to King Jesus.

THE BOTTOM LINE

Your sins have been paid for. Prepare for the Lord!

→ TAKE IT FURTHER

Get on the highway to page 116.

32 | Fade away

Men are like grass and Christians are like sheep, according to Isaiah. What is he talking about??? Let's find out.

 Read Isaiah 40 v 6–8

ENGAGE YOUR BRAIN

▷ *What are people and their achievements ("glory") compared to? (v6)*

▷ *What happens to them? (v7)*

▷ *But what lasts forever? (v8)*

We decay and fade away, as do all our possessions and achievements. But God's word never changes; it stands for ever and can be fully relied upon. The only thing we can rest our hopes on is the only thing that will truly last — a relationship with everlasting God. We can totally trust Him and His word.

Read verses 9–11

▷ *What's the great news for God's people? (v9–10)*

▷ *How does the Lord treat His people? (v11)*

The good news must be shouted out! The Lord Jesus will come with the power of a mighty warrior and with the care of a shepherd looking after his sheep. Just as God would rescue the people of Jerusalem from exile in foreign countries — Jesus rescues His people from God's punishment and brings them home to Himself. Amazing.

SHARE IT

▷ *How are verses 6–11 comforting for Christians?*

▷ *How can you use them to encourage a believer you know?*

PRAY ABOUT IT

Use verse 11 as the focus of your prayers today.

THE BOTTOM LINE

The word of our God stands for ever.

→ TAKE IT FURTHER

Don't fade away. Go to page 116.

33 No comparison

God's people had rejected Him for centuries and yet He promised to bring them back to Himself, forgiven. Superb. But could God's people know this for sure? Yes, with a reminder of how incomparable God is.

👁 **Read Isaiah 40 v 12–14**

ENGAGE YOUR BRAIN
Answer the questions in v12–14.

🔼 *What's the point being made?*

👁 **Read verses 15–20**

🔼 *How do mighty nations compare with God? (v15–17)*
🔼 *Why is worshipping anything else ridiculously stupid? (v18–20)*

👁 **Read verses 21–26**

🔼 *How do we compare to God? (v22)*
🔼 *What about powerful rulers? (v23–24)*
🔼 *What does God do? (v22, v26)*
🔼 *What does this tell us about God?*

👁 **Read verses 27–31**

🔼 *Despite all they knew about almighty God, how did His people treat Him? (v27)*
🔼 *What did they need to realise? (v28)*

🔼 *Have you really understood this yourself?*
🔼 *How should it affect the way you treat God?*
🔼 *What does God do for those who trust in Him? (v29, v31)*

Given the astonishing facts of v12–26, how could God's people complain about Him??? It's madness to whine about God, yet we often live as if we think we could do things better. Crazy. The Lord is the one who creates, sustains, controls and directs His world for His purposes. And He's promised to restore and renew His people. Who can compare to Him?

PRAY ABOUT IT
Read through today's Bible bit again, using it to praise God and confess your failings.

THE BOTTOM LINE
No one compares to God.

➡ **TAKE IT FURTHER**
More incomparable stuff on p116.

34 | Courtroom drama

Imagine a huge courtroom with representatives from every nation there. God is in the dock and has been asked to prove He's really in charge of the world. Here's His evidence...

👁 Read Isaiah 41 v 1–7

ENGAGE YOUR BRAIN

▷ How does God compare to mighty nations? (v2–4)

▷ What was the pointless alternative to trusting God? (v5–7)

Faith in idols and fake gods is stupid. As is trusting in nations and authorities — God controls them and can wipe them out at will. Nothing and no one comes anywhere close to having God's strength and power.

👁 Read verses 8–20

▷ In what different ways are God's people (Israel) described? (v8, v14, v17)

▷ What did God promise them?
v10:
v15:
v17:

▷ Why would God do all these things? (v20)

👁 Read verses 21–29

▷ What challenges did God lay down? (v22–23)

▷ What was God's verdict on idols and idol worshippers? (v24)

▷ What was the sad truth for those who rejected God? (v28–29)

Fake gods can't do anything. No gods can help or guide us except the Lord. It's stupid to put your trust in anything but God. He controls nations and does incredible things for His people — He can and and should be trusted completely. He's in charge.

THINK IT OVER

▷ How will all this help you when you feel deserted by God?

▷ What do you need to remember?

→ TAKE IT FURTHER
More drama on page 116.

35 | God's servant

Yesterday we heard God's promise to raise up a conqueror who'd do battle to benefit God's people. That was King Cyrus of Persia. Today God's talking about raising up someone even more impressive.

👁 Read Isaiah 42 v 1–4

ENGAGE YOUR BRAIN

▶ What would God do for this servant? (v1)

▶ What would this servant do?
v1:
v3:
v4:

▶ What wouldn't he do?
v2:
v3:
v4:

What a servant! He'd be gentle yet tough. He'd bring justice to the world — ensuring nations recognised the Lord as their Creator and Ruler.

👁 Read verses 5–9

▶ How is God described? (v5)

▶ What's His relationship to the servant? (v6)

▶ What would God send the servant to do? (v6–7)

▶ Why can God be trusted? (v5, v8–9)

God's answer to His people's failure and weakness is a real person. Someone who would reverse the situation (v7), act gently (v2–3) and determinedly (v4), bring God's word to the world (v1) and offer hope (v4). Brilliant! No prizes for working out that Jesus is this servant.

THINK IT OVER

▶ How do Isaiah's words help us grasp what Jesus did?

▶ What's your reaction to all this?

PRAY ABOUT IT

Pick at least three things from v1–9 to praise and thank God for.

→ TAKE IT FURTHER

Self service – go to page 117.

36 | Songs and wrongs

There are contrasting emotions in today's chunk of Isaiah: God's people are full of joy and praise; God is positive about the future too; but He's also frustrated by the way His people have treated Him. An emotional rollercoaster.

Read Isaiah 42 v 10–17

ENGAGE YOUR BRAIN

▶ Who will sing this new song praising God? (v10–11)

▶ What were they looking forward to? (v13)

Previously, God made Himself known mainly to His own people, Israel. But now, through His servant (Jesus), He would reach the whole world.

▶ What would He do for them? (v16)

▶ What did they need to do? (v17)

Read verses 18–25

▶ How does God describe His people, Israel? (v18)

▶ Why? (v20, v24)

▶ So what did God do? (v25)

▶ Amazingly, how did they respond? (end of v25)

Hideous stuff. They'd received truth direct from God, but ignored it. And rebelled against it (v24). Instead of Israel reaching the world, the world invaded Israel (v22). And, frighteningly, God's people had no spiritual grasp of what was going on (v25).

GET ON WITH IT

▶ In what ways are you blind and deaf to God and His word?

▶ What will you do about it?

PRAY ABOUT IT

Instead of ignoring God, we should be singing His praises — telling others about Him; and also in prayer directly to Him. Use verses 10–17 as a starting point for your "song" to the Lord.

→ TAKE IT FURTHER

A little bit more on page 117.

37 | The one and only

Israel were described as being blind and deaf —
ignoring the truth and rebelling against God.
We all know what they deserved, but God always
surprises us with His incredible compassion.

👁 Read Isaiah 43 v 1–7

ENGAGE YOUR BRAIN

▶ *Despite their rebellion, what
was still God's relationship to
His people? (v3)*

▶ *What had He done for them
in the past? (v1)*

▶ *What would He do for them in
the future? (v2, v5)*

▶ *Why? (v4, v7)*

This is how God treats His people
despite the way they've treated Him.
Incredible. Read through these verses
again, carefully. Think about which
of these words are true for Christians
today. Then tell God how you feel
about that.

👁 Read verses 8–13

▶ *What does the Lord declare
about Himself?*
v10:
v11:

v12:
v13:

Israel was surrounded by mighty
enemies. So God was reassuring them
that they didn't need to be afraid
— He was with them to bring them
through tough times. He had created
them and chosen them. They had the
one and only God on their side!

SHARE IT

▶ *How can you use today's verses
to explain your relationship with
God?*

PRAY ABOUT IT

After today's astonishing truths,
it's time to praise God. Big time.

THE BOTTOM LINE

God is the one and only.

→ TAKE IT FURTHER

Time to psing a psalm on page 117.

38 | What's in a name?

All of these names describe God in today's verses: The Lord; your Redeemer; the Holy One of Israel; your King; your Holy One; Israel's Creator. Another good name for God is the Rescuer...

👁 Read Isaiah 43 v 14–21

ENGAGE YOUR BRAIN

▶ What would God do? (v14)

▶ Why? (v15)

▶ How could they be sure He'd do this? (16–17)

And if the prospect of months of risky travel through the desert back to a wrecked Jerusalem was terrifying...

▶ What encouragement was there for them? (v19–21)

👁 Read verses 22–28

▶ Where had God's people gone seriously wrong? (v22–24)

▶ What would be the punishment? (v28)

▶ Yet what would God do for those who turned back to Him? (v25)

👁 Read Isaiah 44 v 1–5

▶ What had God done in the past? (v2)

▶ And what would He do in the future? (v2)

▶ What does He give to His people? (v3)

▶ What could these people call themselves? (v5)

God would forgive our murky past (and not let that determine how He treats us) and give us the ability to live for Him — His Spirit living in us. Huge promises! And there would be no need any longer to fear His judgment (v2).

PRAY ABOUT IT

As you talk to God today, use Isaiah 44 v 1–5 to inform the way you pray.

➡ TAKE IT FURTHER

A tiny bit more on page 117.

39 | Idol talk

**What things and "gods" do people worship?
What are you tempted to idolise?
Today, God shows up the foolishness
of worshipping anything but Him.**

👁 **Read Isaiah 44 v 6–8**

ENGAGE YOUR BRAIN

▶ *What's today's description of God? (v6)*

▶ *So... who is like God? (v8)*

👁 **Read verses 9–20**

▶ *What does God say about idols?*
v9:
v15–17:
v18:

▶ *What does He say about idol makers?*
v9:
v10:
v12–15

▶ *And what about people who stood up for false gods?*
v9:
v18:
v19:
v20:

It's ludicrous to carve something from a lump of firewood and treat it as God. But any idol we create (and devote ourselves to) actually ends up deceiving, blinding and controlling us.

👁 **Read verses 21–23**

▶ *What truth should shape Israel's future behaviour? (v21–22)*

▶ *Why is this response the right one? (v23)*

GET ON WITH IT

▶ *What idols do you need to throw away?*

▶ *How can you (sensitively) stand up for your belief in the one true God when friends share their non-Christian beliefs?*

PRAY ABOUT IT

Talk to God about what's on your mind today.

➔ **TAKE IT FURTHER**

Don't be idle, go to page 117.

51

Cyrus the conqueror

Through Isaiah, God announced a two-part plan: to rescue His people from Babylon and to rescue them from sin. Part one involves a conqueror; part two involves a servant. Let's start with part one — the conqueror.

👁 Read Isaiah 44 v 24–28

ENGAGE YOUR BRAIN

▶ *What evidence does God give that He keeps His word?*
v24:
v25:
v26:
v27:

▶ *Who would God use to rescue His people from Babylon? (v28)*

▶ *What would happen to dilapidated Jerusalem? (v28)*

👁 Read Isaiah 45 v 1–13

▶ *How would God help Cyrus in his task? (v1–3)*

▶ *Why? (v3, v4, v6)*

▶ *Yet how did Cyrus respond to God? (v4)*

▶ *Why shouldn't anyone complain at God's way of doing things? (v9–12)*

▶ *What would God use Cyrus to do? (v13)*

Surprisingly, God would use this idol-worshipping, Persian bully to take God's people back to Jerusalem and rebuild God's city and temple. Cyrus would achieve this with God's help (v2), for the sake of God's people (v4), so that everyone would know that the Lord is the one true God (v6).

PRAY ABOUT IT

All we can do when faced with such an impressive God is worship Him. Go through today's reading, verse by verse, praising God for who He is and what He's done.

→ TAKE IT FURTHER

No *Take it further* today.

41 Poetic truth

Cyrus and the Persians were impressive, conquering everyone in their path. But they were weak and pathetic compared to Almighty God, who was in control. Isaiah wrote a poem about Him...

Read Isaiah 45 v 14–17

ENGAGE YOUR BRAIN

- God's people were captives, but what could they look forward to? (v14)

- What will happen to the idol makers we read about? (v16)

- What was the great news for God's people? (v17)

The world would submit to Israel's God — some willingly, who'd be rescued (v17), and some unwillingly, who wouldn't (v16).

Read verses 18–21

- List some of God's qualities from these verses:

Read verses 22–25

- What is God's great invitation? (v22)

- What are the only two ways to respond?

- What will everyone do, eventually? (end of v23)

One day, everyone will submit to God as their ruler, whether they want to or not (v23). You can rage all you like, it will make no difference.

THINK IT OVER

- What's your response to v22?

PRAY ABOUT IT

Pray for people you know (maybe yourself?) who refuse to accept God's invitation. Pray they'll realise that it's pointless to rage against God — everyone will bow down to Him in the end. Pray that they'll choose to do so before it's too late and they're forced to.

→ TAKE IT FURTHER

More poetry on page 118.

42 | Shock result

God's people were conquered by Babylon and many of them were taken away to live there. The situation must have seemed hopeless. But God had some big news about Babylon.

👁 Read Isaiah 46 v 1–7

ENGAGE YOUR BRAIN

- ▷ What will happen to the gods and idols of Babylon? (v1)
- ▷ What's the news for God's people stuck in Babylon? (v3–4)
- ▷ What's the answer to v5?
- ▷ What's the news for people who worship other gods? (v6–7)

👁 Read verses 8–13

- ▷ What must "rebels" remember? (v8–10)
- ▷ What surprise did God have in store for Babylon? (v11–13)
- ▷ How would this be great for God's people? (v13)

👁 Read Isaiah 47 v 1–15

- ▷ How was Babylon described? (v1–3)
- ▷ What would happen to this mighty, godless nation? (v5, v9, v11)
- ▷ Why? (v6–8, v10)
- ▷ What would happen to Babylon's sorcerers/astrologers? (v12–15)

Nothing compares to God, so there's no point living for anyone or anything else. The Babylonians would eventually realise that there's only one God and He could do as He pleased (v10) — including bringing about Babylon's destruction.

And that's what we all need to realise — there's only one God and if we choose to ignore Him, we're in big trouble. So we must stop worshipping idols (money, popularity, success, sex etc), ignore horoscopes and fortune-tellers, and serve the living God.

PRAY ABOUT IT
Talk to God. You know what you need to say.

→ TAKE IT FURTHER
No *Take it further* today.

43 | Fools freed

Remember God's two-part rescue plan? Part one involves a conqueror and part two involves a servant. Well, we're still on part one, and it's bad news for Babylon. Not that Israel was perfect...

Read Isaiah 48 v 1–11

ENGAGE YOUR BRAIN

▶ Who does God summon? (v1–2)

▶ What does He say about them? (v4, v8)

▶ Why would God stick with these stubborn people? (v9–11)

The world must know that God is in charge, not Babylon or any idols. So God presses on with His perfect plans, even though His people are useless most of the time.

Read verses 12–22

▶ What did God tell His gathered people? (v13–14)

▶ What would King Cyrus of Persia do? (v14–15)

▶ How would life have been better if God's people had obeyed Him? (v18–19)

▶ Why should they praise God? (v20–21)

Why would God bother to rescue *these* people? They were pig-headed, twisting the truth, blind to evidence, grumbling, deceitful, ungodly and obsessed by idols. Shockingly, it's these people who God would rescue!

But a change of scene wouldn't mean a change of heart: God's people were returning to Jerusalem, but not returning to God. It would need someone greater than Cyrus to sort God's people out. Someone like the guy in 48 v 16. More about him tomorrow.

PRAY ABOUT IT

Thank God for sticking by His promises when His people don't. That's truly amazing grace.

→ TAKE IT FURTHER

Find some more on page 118.

44 | Light relief

God would use Cyrus to rescue His rebel people from exile in Babylon. But it needed someone far greater than Cyrus to deal with their sin.

👁 Read Isaiah 49 v 1–7

▶ *What qualified this "servant" to rescue God's people?*
v1:
v2:
v3:
v5:

▶ *What extra mission would God give His servant? (v6)*

▶ *How would people respond? (v7)*
At first:
Later:

A figure born as a human, but set apart by God (v1), who'd speak powerfully (v2), reveal God's glory (v3) when the time was right, go through dark times but trust God (v4–5). And transform Israel, then the world, with His rescue (v6). He'd be rejected by His own people, yet everyone will bow down to Him in the end (v7).

👁 Read verses 8–13

▶ *What would the servant do for God's people? (v8–9)*

▶ *What else? (v10)*

▶ *What's the only right response? (v13)*

God's people would no longer be a small nation: they'd be a worldwide people. God's perfect servant, Jesus, would rescue them and restore their relationship with God. News like that should make us all get on our rooftops and sing!

PRAY ABOUT IT

List what we learn about Jesus in these verses:

Include those things in a praise prayer (or song) to Him.

→ TAKE IT FURTHER

Covenant question on page 118.

45 | Forgiven, not forgotten

Yesterday we heard how God's people would be rescued and there would be huge celebrations. But for God's people stuck in Babylon, everything seemed hopeless.

👁 **Read Isaiah 49 v 14–21**

ENGAGE YOUR BRAIN

ⓘ *What did the people of Zion/Jerusalem claim? (v14)*

ⓘ *What was God's great response? (v15–16)*

ⓘ *How would things change for God's people? (v17–19)*

Yet again, God's people were ignoring the facts. They felt abandoned yet they should know that God always rescues His people. Like a mother can't forget her baby, God would never forget His people (v15). Like a proud father spoiling his daughter on her wedding day, God would give His people so much (v18). The new Jerusalem would be far greater than anyone could imagine (v19–21). God's love for His people is extravagant and neverending.

👁 **Read verses 22–26**

ⓘ *Who else would be included in God's people? (v22)*

ⓘ *What would Israel's enemies do? (v23)*

ⓘ *What would this prove? (v23)*

ⓘ *What would happen to Israel's (and God's) enemies? (v24–26)*

ⓘ *What will everyone eventually realise? (v26)*

The whole world has a decision to make. Either submit to God and become part of His people, or go against God and His people and face the terrifying consequences.

PRAY ABOUT IT

Pray for those close to you who reject and God and His people. If you're a believer, thank God that He is your Redeemer, Saviour and Mighty God.

➡ **TAKE IT FURTHER**

Don't forget to turn to page 118.

A changed life

What was life like for you as a student?

When I was at university my main aim was to have fun. It was all about me! I lived a life I thought would make me happy. So my life was more and more centered around alcohol, sex and drugs. If you'd asked me, I'd have said I was a Christian; but I didn't think about God much, and God definitely wasn't part of my everyday life.

Most people around me would have said I was happy. But as I approached the end of my course, I was totally unsatisfied. I knew my ideas of how to bring myself real joy had failed. All the things I'd focused on were short term and hadn't really given me much happiness or purpose. Looking back at my past lifestyle now, to be honest it seems pointless and stupid.

How did you become a Christian?

When I finished university, I moved back home and got a job. My parents had always been to church, so I went along with them. That's how I started to really think about Christianity.

I began to read the Bible. For so long I'd been relying on my own "wisdom", but as I read the Bible I got to know Jesus. My understanding of what life was all about began to change! God gently challenged me about the lifestyle I was living.

I was in a relationship and I was doing things that weren't obedient to Christ. On a weekend away with my church, I got to the stage where I knew things had to change and I couldn't carry on going out with this girl. It wasn't because we'd fallen out or didn't get along; but I knew that I was using the relationship to avoid facing the reality of becoming a Christian. So I ended it.

For me, there wasn't a "light-bulb moment" where I became a Christian — it happened slowly. But over a few months, I realised that lasting joy is what I can get from knowing Jesus. I discovered that He knows me personally, more deeply than even I do — and that He died and rose to take my sins and forgive me.

What's changed in your lifestyle?

My perspective on life and everything I do has changed. My main aim now is to be more like Jesus, as the Holy Spirit changes me. So practically, I don't drink heavily, take drugs or run after girls any more. I've given a lot up: but looking back I can say with full confidence that the change in my life is certainly for the better.

I don't think I'm an extreme example — lots of people are in a similar position. But any life lived without God at the centre is a mistake — if we don't know God and love God, we'll never find real joy, love or purpose in life.

What's hard about being a Christian?

Standing up for Christianity in a world which sees my faith as outdated or ridiculous is challenging. I have lost friends because I've become a Christian and won't get involved with what they're doing. It can be hard to spend time with friends who aren't Christians: and I'm often shamed that I don't stand up for Jesus more than I do. It's a real challenge to discuss a Christian perspective on things when it often appears stupid to them.

Given your experience of uni, would you suggest avoiding it?

No — I don't want to scare anyone away from going to university! But you do need to be careful, and remember that since God created us, He knows us best and He knows the best way for us to live. I'd say make sure you join a good church, and a Christian group. Make some good Christian friends, who you can look to for advice, and who'll challenge you when you need it.

And remember where joy really comes from. I know now that my ultimate joy will be when I see Jesus face to face — I have every good thing to look forward to in the new creation. I couldn't have said that two years ago, and now I can — thank God!

Chris Shepherd was interviewed for engage *by Carl Laferton.*

Acts

Under pressure

Acts has told us the story of Paul, the persecutor of Christians; Paul, the planter of churches; and now, in the last eight chapters, it's the story of Paul, the prisoner in chains.

We're going to follow Paul, who Jesus converted from one of His greatest enemies to one of His greatest workers as Paul walked along a road to Damascus (read about it in Acts 9). We'll see him under pressure — serious pressure. Will he lose his faith in God? Will he shut up about Jesus? As he travels to Jerusalem, and then on to Rome, will loneliness, imprisonment, danger, deceit and shipwreck stop Him following Christ? As we read these words of Luke (who was an eyewitness of many of the events he tells us about), we're not only finding out about Paul, though. We're also finding out about Jesus, the Son of God, who keeps His promises even when His people are under pressure.

And we're finding out about life as a follower of Jesus today. In watching how Paul the prisoner reacts to scrapes, setbacks and sadnesses, we can learn how Jesus wants His followers today to act when we find ourselves under pressure. So let's get back on the road with Paul...

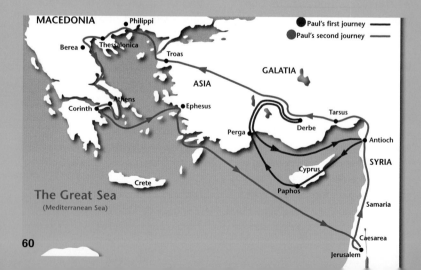

46 | Christian sense

"Better safe than sorry." "Common sense is vital." "Don't take risks." It's all good advice, but are they the final word for the Christian? Is that how believers should live?

ENGAGE YOUR BRAIN

▶ Look back to Acts 19 v 21. Where's Paul decided to visit?

👁 Read Acts 21 v 1–12

▶ List the verses in which Paul is advised not to go to Jerusalem:

▶ Who is speaking to him in each of these verses?

▶ Why do they advise him to change his mind? (v11)

▶ Which words show how concerned they were?

👁 Read 21 v 13–16

▶ Does Paul change his mind? Why / why not?

▶ How do his friends respond? (v14–15)

THINK IT THROUGH

▶ What would common sense say about Paul's plan to go to Jerusalem?

And that's what his friends say to him. They're not wrong to do this; there's a place for sensible advice — but sensible advice doesn't have the last word for the Christian.

▶ What should our attitude be when we're called to do something risky for Jesus? (v13)

▶ What should be our response when a Christian friend decides to take a risk for Jesus? (v14)

GET ON WITH IT

▶ Is there an area of your life where you're being sensible, but it's stopping you living 100% for Jesus?

▶ How does this section challenge you to change?

THE BOTTOM LINE

Being sensible is good; but it must not stop us taking risks for Jesus.

➔ TAKE IT FURTHER

It makes sense to go to page 118.

Bending over backwards

This is quite a tricky section, because Paul seems to do things that he's told others in Acts and his letters not to do — so we'll need to look hard at what we're actually being taught.

Read Acts 21 v 17–26

▶ *Where's Paul? (v17)*

▶ *How do the Christians there react to him and what God's been doing through him? (v17–20)*

But people have been hearing dangerous things about Paul...

▶ *What have some Jewish Christians been told? (v21)*

The issue here is whether Paul's been telling Jews who've become Christians to turn their backs on their Jewish heritage and culture.

▶ *What's the solution Paul's Christian friends in Jerusalem suggest? (v22–24)*

▶ *What does Paul do?*

▶ *He's not doing this because he has to, to be a Christian — so what's his motivation for doing it?*

Read Acts 21 v 27–36

Paul's done everything he can to ensure Christianity doesn't have a bad name.

▶ *How do the people respond?*

▶ *What do they want to do? (v 31)*

THINK ABOUT IT
Read Romans 12 v 17–18
Paul's practising what he preached. He's bent over backwards to live at peace with everyone around him — but it isn't possible, because the people around him have rejected his gospel message and are determined to see the worst in him.

GET ON WITH IT
What have you learned about how you should live among friends and family who don't believe the gospel?

→ TAKE IT FURTHER
Go round the bend to page 118.

48 But seriously...

If you're really serious about God and knowing Him, what will you do? That's what Paul wants the people who are trying to kill him to think about.

👁 Read Acts 21 v 37 – 22 v 2

ENGAGE YOUR BRAIN

▶ What does Paul ask the Roman commander? (v 39)

▶ Based on what you know of Paul, what do you think Paul will want to talk to them about?

👁 Read Acts 22 v 3–9

▶ How does Paul introduce himself (v 3)?

▶ Why, do you think?

▶ What does Paul say about his attitude to God? (end v 3)

"Zealous" means "seriously serious". Paul was serious about the whole God thing: and these people think they are, too.

▶ What did Paul think being zealous for God meant he needed to do? (v 4–5)

▶ What was his relationship to Jesus? (v 7–8)

But when Jesus appeared to him and spoke to him as he travelled to Damascus, he realised that he'd misunderstood how to be serious about following God.

👁 Read Acts 22 v 10–21

▶ If someone's really serious about knowing God, what must they do? (v 15–16)

THE BOTTOM LINE

Taking God seriously means talking about Christ, not persecuting Him.

GET ON WITH IT

▶ Who do you know who say they take God seriously, but push Jesus out instead of living for Him?

▶ How can you explain to them how to take God seriously?

→ TAKE IT FURTHER

I'm serious — turn to page 119.

49 : So many voices

Ever felt surrounded by so many people talking to and at you that you don't know what to do or who to listen to?

👁 Read Acts 22 v 21–29

ENGAGE YOUR BRAIN
▷ *What does Paul tell the crowd Jesus had told him to do? (v21)*
▷ *How do the crowd react? (v22)*

Telling people about Jesus can be met with anger and hostility. The message is: don't tell us about Jesus!

👁 Read Acts 22 v 30 – 23 v 5
Paul's hauled up before the Jewish religious court which had condemned Jesus to death, flogged the disciples Peter and John, and killed the Christian Stephen.

▷ *What does Paul say to them? (v1)*

In other words: I've done nothing wrong, because my duty to God is to follow Jesus and spread His message.

▷ *What does the high priest say in response? (v2)*
▷ *What's his message to Paul about living for Christ?*

👁 Read Acts 23 v 6–11
▷ *What does Paul say about why he's on trial? (v 6)*
▷ *How do the Sadducees respond, and why? (v 7–10)*
▷ *What's the Sadducees' message to Paul about believing in the risen Christ?*
▷ *Who comes and speaks to Paul? (v11)*
▷ *What's His message to Paul about how he's preaching and living?*

THE BOTTOM LINE
There are lots of voices with different messages; all that matters is Jesus' voice.

PRAY ABOUT IT
Lord Jesus, Help me to listen to your word in the Bible and to ignore people who tell me to stop speaking about you, living for you, or believing in you. Amen.

→ TAKE IT FURTHER
More encouragement on page 119.

50 | We'll kill him!

Paul's in serious trouble. The Jewish leaders hate him; the crowd wants to kill him; the Roman authorities don't know what to do with him.

👁 **Read Acts 23 v 12–24**

ENGAGE YOUR BRAIN

▷ *What's shocking about v12?*

▷ *How will the plan work? (v 13-15)*

▷ *Why doesn't the plan work? (v16–24)*

👁 **Read Acts 23 v 25–35**

The commander, Lysias, writes a letter to his boss, Governor Felix, about Paul.

▷ *What does the commander miss out of the story? (v 27–30: compare it with 22 v 22–29)*

▷ *Why do you think he changes the details a bit?*

THINK IT THROUGH

Paul's protected by a man who wants to use him to look good from a bunch of men who want to kill him to shut him up. No one actually cares about him. It must have been seriously

lonely and hugely terrifying.

▷ *Look back to 23 v 11. How would this have encouraged Paul?*

And behind the scenes of this passage He is working to ensure that His plan happens.

PRAY ABOUT IT

In our world right now thousands of Christians are being plotted against by those who want to kill them, and are only protected by authorities when it suits them. Pray for these Christians now, that they'd remember Jesus is in charge, and that He'll look after them until it is time for them to join Him in eternal life.

THE BOTTOM LINE

No matter what those around you are doing, trust in Jesus for your life and your death.

➡ **TAKE IT FURTHER**

More stuff on page 119.

51 | Court-ing controversy

We're in court. The judge: Roman governor Felix.
The prosecution: Jewish religious leaders.
The accused: Christian missionary Paul.
The punishment if found guilty: death.

👁 Read Acts 24 v 1–9

ENGAGE YOUR BRAIN

▶ What does the prosecution lawyer accuse Paul of?

If true, Paul hadn't only broken Jewish religious laws; he'd also broken Roman state laws.

▶ What do the witnesses say? (v9)

👁 Read Acts 24 v 10–21

▶ How does Paul defend himself from the accusations?

▶ What's the one thing he wants to admit publicly? (v14)

The Way = Christianity.

👁 Read Acts 24 v 22–27

The governor chickens out! He knows Paul isn't guilty, but he knows the Jews will cause trouble if he says that: so he leaves Paul in prison for two years.

▶ What happens while Paul's in prison? (v24)

Drusilla was a stunner. She'd been married to another ruler, but had left him for Felix. It had caused a huge scandal.

▶ What does Paul tell them about? (v24–25)

Seriously brave. Paul talked about self-control to a couple who had failed to resist their adulterous urges! Paul talked about the judgment to come to two powerful figures who were facing that judgment. Paul's happy to defend himself against untruth to save his life; but he'll always risk his life to tell people the truth about God's judgment, our sin, and Christ's rescue.

GET ON WITH IT

▶ Who can you take a risk with to talk to about Jesus?

→ TAKE IT FURTHER

More controversy on page 119.

52 | When being offensive is good

Paul's enemies don't give up easily as they try to kill him...
but then, neither does Paul as he tries to talk about Jesus.
It's like a deadly staring match, with the Romans as the
judge. Who'll blink first?

👁 Read Acts 25 v 1–9

It's another trial; the new Roman
governor, Festus, is judge. Again the
Jews, who've had another murderous
plot foiled (v3–5), bring "many
serious charges against him" (v7).

▷ *What's the basic message of
Paul's defence? (v8)*

▷ *Is he guilty of wrongdoing under
either Jewish or Roman law?*

▷ *Festus, like the other Romans,
wants to use Paul for his own
ends — so what does he ask
Paul to do? (v9)*

▷ *Why's this a problem for Paul?
(look back to v3)*

In the end, Paul ends up heading
for Rome, not Jerusalem (v 12 —
see *Take It Further*).

👁 Read Acts 25 v 13–22

▷ *Who appears on the scene? (v13)*

▷ *What does Festus tell them the
whole argument between Paul
and the Jews boils down to? (v19)*

▷ *What has Paul clearly still been
talking about loads?*

THINK ABOUT IT

▷ *Paul's obeyed the law; he's
obeyed the leaders of the state;
he's obeyed local traditions;
what's the one way he's caused
offence?*

▷ *Will he stop?*

GET ON WITH IT

▷ *How's this an encouragement
and challenge to you?*

THE BOTTOM LINE

Whatever happens, keep talking
about a "dead man" named Jesus
who you know is alive.

→ TAKE IT FURTHER

More offensive words on page 119.

53 Christianity on trial

"How can you be a Christian and intelligent?" "What about other religions?" "Why do you have to take it so seriously?" Sound familiar? Let's see how Paul answers.

👁 Read Acts 25 v 23–27

Agrippa II ruled part of Israel. His great-grandfather, Herod, tried to kill Jesus when he was born. His grandfather, Herod Antipas, killed John the Baptist. His father, Herod Agrippa I, beheaded Jesus' apostle James. Not a nice family!

👁 Read Acts 26 v 1–23

ENGAGE YOUR BRAIN

- ▶ *What job had Jesus given Paul? (v15–18)*
- ▶ *So, had Paul forgotten about the Jewish Scriptures (the Old Testament), and all the promises God had made in them? (v6–7)*
- ▶ *What's Paul saying about how the Old Testament links to Jesus?*
- ▶ *What does v 22-23 add?*

THINK IT THROUGH

- ▶ *How would you explain the gospel to someone who's been brought up as a Jew?*
- ▶ *What point does Paul make in v8?*

- ▶ *What would you say to someone who thinks there might be a God, but thinks Christian belief is stupid?*
- ▶ *Jesus had called Paul to live for him (v 16–18); how did Paul respond (v19–20)?*
- ▶ *What had this resulted in? (v21)*

Paul obeyed Jesus. He went and told the world that Jesus had risen, even though he risked death by doing it. When Jesus calls you to follow Him, you can't half-obey; it requires 100% commitment.

PRAY ABOUT IT

Lord Jesus, Thank you that you're the One all God's promises came true through. Thank you that you've called me to be forgiven, be part of your people, and serve you with my life. Amen.

→ TAKE IT FURTHER

More trials on page 120.

54 | Response to a response

There are two responses in today's section: people's response to Paul, and Paul's response to people.

👁 Read Acts 26 v 19–28

ENGAGE YOUR BRAIN

Paul's basic message to the governor and king: God's King, Jesus, suffered, died and rose from the dead to offer the light of eternal life to all (23).

ᐅ *How does Festus respond? (v24)*

Paul asks Agrippa if he believes the Old Testament prophets, who Paul says point to Jesus being God's King.

ᐅ *How does Agrippa respond? (v28)*

The tone here is probably: "You (a prisoner in chains) think you can persuade me (a powerful king) to become a Christian? Ha!"

ᐅ *Which words best describe Festus and Agrippa's response to Paul's message?*

👁 Read Acts 26 v 29–32

ᐅ *What's Paul's response to this sneering king? (v29)*

ᐅ *What does he have that he wants the king to have?*

Paul's amazing here. You'd think his prayer would be "God, please get me out of here alive"; but in fact it's "God, please give these people faith in your Son".

GET ON WITH IT

ᐅ *How does your attitude to your life need to change to be more like Paul's?*

PRAY ABOUT IT

Think of someone you know who sneers at you for being a Christian, and commit to praying for them daily.

THE BOTTOM LINE

People often respond to Christianity by sneering; Christians should respond to them by praying.

→ TAKE IT FURTHER

Quick response — page 120.

55 When times get tough

Ever had a day, a week, or even a year, when everything just goes wrong? What's God doing in those times? How should you react?

WHEN IT ALL GOES WRONG...

👁 Read Acts 27 v 1–12

ENGAGE YOUR BRAIN

Paul's going to Rome: but by the end of v 8 they've only reached Crete, less than halfway.

▶ What's the problem? (v9)
▶ What does Paul advise? (v 9–10)
▶ What decision is made? (v12)

👁 Read verses 13–20

▶ What happens at sea?
▶ The ship's crew try everything; but by v20, how's everybody feeling?

Luke says "we" — even Paul's Christian friends felt like this.

...LISTEN TO GOD'S PROMISES...

👁 Read 27 v 21–26

▶ What's Paul been told? (v23–24)
▶ So what does he tell everyone to do? (v25)

...AND TRUST IN THEM

Notice that Paul doesn't just know what God's said: crucially, he trusts God to do what He's said.

THINK ABOUT IT

▶ What had God promised Paul twice now? (23 v 11, 27 v 24)
▶ Did God at any stage promise Paul that life would be easy along the way?

GET ON WITH IT

God hasn't promised all Christians He'll get them to Rome; but He has promised to get them to eternal life.

▶ What have you learned about what to do when everything in life seems to be going wrong?

THE BOTTOM LINE

Keep up your courage; have faith that things will happen just as God has told you.

→ TAKE IT FURTHER

The tough get going... to page 120.

56 | Put your feet up?

Paul is trusting God to keep His promise to get him to Rome. So now Paul can just relax, put his feet up, and wait for God to sort it all out, right? Err...wrong, actually.

👁 Read Acts 27 v 27–32

ENGAGE YOUR BRAIN
▶ What do the sailors do? (v30)

This would stop anyone getting to Rome!

▶ What does Paul do? (v31–32)

Problem solved — the Rome trip's still on!

👁 Read 27 v 33–38
▶ What's the problem? (v33)
▶ What does Paul do? (v34–36)

Problem solved — Rome's still on!

👁 Read 27 v 39–44
▶ What do the soldiers intend to do? (v42)
▶ What does the centurion do, and why? (v43–44)

Paul hasn't solved this problem directly — and yet the centurion "wanted to spare Paul's life", probably because Paul had been such a help to him during the storm. Anyway, problem solved — Rome's still on!

THINK ABOUT IT
▶ Does trusting in God's promises mean we don't work hard to keep things on track ourselves?
▶ Does working hard mean we don't need to trust in God to make His promises come true?

After all, God usually works through His people to make His promises come true! Think of one aspect of your life where you need to trust in God's promises and work hard yourself.

THE BOTTOM LINE
Christians trust God will make His promises come true; then get on with working to make them come true.

→ TAKE IT FURTHER
Don't put your feet up: turn to p120.

57 | Can you believe it?

When people don't believe in God, they'll believe in anything.

👁 Read Acts 28 v 1–4

ENGAGE YOUR BRAIN

- ▶ *Where have Paul and the others ended up? (v1)*
- ▶ *What happens to Paul? (v2–3)*
- ▶ *What do the islanders conclude about Paul, and why? (v4)*
- ▶ *What mistake are they making in their beliefs?*

👁 Read Acts 28 v 5–10

- ▶ *What doesn't happen to Paul? (v5–6)*
- ▶ *What do the islanders conclude about Paul now, and why? (v6)*
- ▶ *What mistake are they making in their beliefs?*
- ▶ *What does Paul go on to do? (v8–9)*
- ▶ *When confronted with the sick man, what does Paul do first? (v8)*
- ▶ *What's he showing about who's in charge?*

THINK ABOUT IT

It's easy to look down on the islanders for what they believed about Paul just because of the snake. But are people so different today? How many people believe the stars affect their personal lives? How many people think doing a certain thing will bring them "luck"? How many people treat someone other than Christ — a boyfriend, or a daughter, or even money or career or sex — as their "god", the thing they worship and would do anything for? Maybe we're not so different…

GET ON WITH IT

- ▶ *Are you treating anything other than Jesus as a "god" in your life?*

Look out for your friends saying something that shows what they believe — it might give you an opportunity to share how your beliefs are different.

THE BOTTOM LINE

When people don't believe in Jesus as God, they'll believe in anything.

→ TAKE IT FURTHER

No *Take it further* today.

58 | Done Rome-in

Which do you think is the world's most important city? What's the world's most exciting city? For people in Paul's time, those questions were easy to answer — Rome, the capital of the largest empire mankind had ever known.

👁 Read Acts 28 v 11–16

ENGAGE YOUR BRAIN

▶ Where does Paul finally end up? (v14)

It was the end of Paul's journey.

▶ Despite all the difficulties in getting there, should we be surprised by this? (Think back to Acts 23 v 11 and 27 v 23–24.)

▶ What kind of situation did Paul find himself in? (v16)

▶ What have we been reminded about God's promises?

▶ What happened when Paul reached Puteoli?

▶ What happened as he approached Rome?

▶ Remember that Paul is a prisoner who may soon be condemned to death — why is the action of the people in v15 surprising?

▶ What does it show about their priorities?

GET ON WITH IT

▶ Do you ever keep quiet when other Christians are sharing the gospel or when your friends are criticising Christianity?

▶ How does this passage encourage you to change?

THE BOTTOM LINE

God's promises always come true; God's people stick up for each other.

→ TAKE IT FURTHER

Roam to Rome on page 120.

59 | The end?

**We've reached the end of Acts (congratulations!)
Is it a happy ending? Sad ending? Unfinished ending?**

👁 Read Acts v 17–24

ENGAGE YOUR BRAIN

▶ Paul's chained to a Roman guard — what does he still want to do? (v20, v23)

▶ What's the response from the Jews (v24)?

👁 Read Acts 28 v 25–31

▶ Who's Paul going to tell about Jesus now?

▶ What does he predict? (v28)

▶ What's Paul doing as the book ends (v30–31)?

This is what Paul's always done, whenever, wherever and however he can. It's a happy ending! Yes — Paul's in Rome, telling people about Jesus. Not sad at all, then? Hmmm... Paul's under house arrest, chained to a guard. God's done great things through Paul, but God hasn't given him an easy life.

So, that's it, finished! Not really... Paul's reached Rome, the centre of the Roman Empire. From Rome, the gospel can go to "the ends of the earth", just as Jesus said way back in Acts 1 v 8. And the gospel's still doing that — as you take it to those you live with, work with, go to school with. The Acts of Jesus, reigning in heaven and working through His people, are not finished yet — and if you're a Christian, you're part of it!

PRAY ABOUT IT

Think of three people you see often who aren't Christians. Ask God for chances to tell them about Christ; ask for the courage and the words when those chances come.

➡ TAKE IT FURTHER

Final Acts on page 120.

60 | Longing for God

Is there something you long for? Maybe a holiday in the sun, or an expensive gadget or certain person you like? Well, this psalm writer was longing to hang out in the temple. Honestly.

◉ Read Psalm 84 v 1–8

ENGAGE YOUR BRAIN

▶ What has got this guy so excited? (v1–2)

▶ Why was he jealous of the birds nesting in God's temple? (v3)

▶ Who is "blessed"? (v4–5)

This man was so excited by God's temple. He wanted to live there so he could be in God's presence. He knew how great it is to be part of God's people (v4–5). Those who trust God and walk with Him (live His way) find help in hard times (v6). And so grow in faith (v7).

◉ Read verses 9–12

▶ What big claim does the writer make? (v10)

▶ What does God do for His people? (v11)

▶ Who are God's people? (v12)

God's people today (Christians) look to Jesus, not a temple. He lives among us. We know He's put us on the way to eternal life — and a place forever in His presence. And we know God doesn't hold anything good back from us, because He gave His Son, Jesus, to die in our place.

GET ON WITH IT

"Blessed" (or favoured) are those who...

• marvel at God's presence as they meet together.
• walk with Him on the road to eternal life.
• trust Him wholeheartedly.

▶ How will this psalm spur you on as a Christian?

PRAY ABOUT IT

Think how you can turn the words of this psalm into a prayer to God that honestly expresses how you feel.

→ TAKE IT FURTHER

Longing for more? Try page 121.

61 | That was then, this is now

This psalm's written when God's people suffered a setback (maybe after God brought His people back to Jerusalem from Babylon — a tough time followed). For once, they turned to the Lord for help.

Read Psalm 85 v 1–7

ENGAGE YOUR BRAIN

▷ *What does this guy remember about God? (v1–3)*

▷ *What had God previously done for His people?*
v1:
v2:
v3:

▷ *So what does He ask God to do now? (v4, v7)*

Since God had shown great mercy to His people in the past, the psalm writer begs God to do it again. He wants God to show His unfailing love and to rescue His people (v7). Ultimately, He did this through Jesus, on the cross.

Read verses 8–13

▷ *What promises from God does he hold on to? (v8–9)*

▷ *Which of God's great qualities*

encourage Him? (v10–13)

What an awesome prospect: God showing His love to a world that rejected Him; remaining faithful to His rebellious people; God's perfect righteousness in harmony with His gift of peace. This will be seen in eternal life, when God's people will live in peace and love and perfection with their faithful God.

PRAY ABOUT IT

Ask God to keep your eyes fixed on a great future with Him. Pray that you'll be faithful to Him in the way you live your life.

→ TAKE IT FURTHER

No *Take it further* today.

62 ¦ Save Dave

This psalm was written by David. You won't be surprised to hear he's in a tight spot again. At least he knows where to turn.

👁 Read Psalm 86 v 1–10

ENGAGE YOUR BRAIN

▶ What does David ask for?
v2:
v3:
v4:

▶ What gives him confidence that God will answer?
v2:
v5:
v8:
v10:

👁 Read verses 11–17

▶ What does David promise to do?
v11:
v12:

▶ Why? (v13)

▶ What's David's big problem? (v14)

▶ What does he ask for? (v17)

▶ Why does he think God will rescue him? (v15–16)

David reminds Himself of what God has done and what He's like. This gives David confidence that God can and will save him. He promises to live God's way and tell everybody how great God is.

GET ON WITH IT

▶ How do you need to walk more in God's truth, living for Him?

▶ How will you glorify God more publicly?

PRAY ABOUT IT

Now tell the Lord about anything that's getting you down right now. Praise Him for who He is and what He's done. Ask God to help you live more for Him and glorify His name.

→ TAKE IT FURTHER

A little more background on p121.

TOOLBOX

Tone and feel

One of the main ambitions of **engage** is to encourage you to dive into God's word and learn how to handle it and understand it more. Each issue, TOOLBOX gives you tips, tools and advice for wrestling with the Bible. This issue, we investigate how the tone and feel of a passage take effect.

WORDS WITH FEELING

There's more to language than merely stating facts. The way words are used and combined has the power to affect the way we feel.

When C.S. Lewis was asked for advice on becoming a better writer, he said: "Instead of telling us a thing is 'terrible', describe it so that we'll be terrified. Don't say 'it was a delight', make us say 'delightful' when we've read the description."

The Bible often uses language to convey feeling in powerful ways. Check out these fearsome words from Ezekiel:

This is what the Sovereign Lord says: "Disaster! An unheard-of disaster is coming. The end has come! The end has come! It has roused itself against you. It has come! Doom has come upon you — you who dwell in the land. The time has come, the day is near; there is panic, not joy, upon the mountains. I am about to pour out my wrath on you and spend my anger against you ...

The day is here! It has come! Doom has burst forth, the rod has budded, arrogance has blossomed! Violence has grown into a rod to punish wickedness; none of the people will be left, none of that crowd — no wealth, nothing of value. The time has come, the day has arrived."
(Ezekiel 7 v 5–12)

If all Ezekiel had wanted to do was state a fact, then simply saying "Judgment Day is here" would have done the job. But it wouldn't have had the same powerful impact.

78

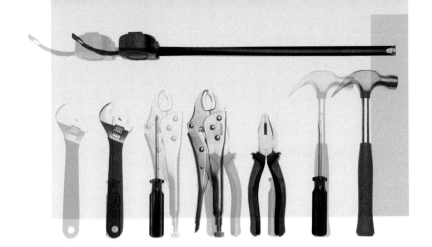

WORDS WITH EFFECT

When we come to the Bible, we should pay attention not only to the point that is being made (though that is the first priority), but also exactly how it's being made. We need to be alert to the author's tone, to immerse ourselves in the picture he paints in such a way that our imaginations are awakened and our emotions are engaged. Think to yourself: what does the writer want me to feel as I read this?

We shouldn't read the Bible as if it's a boring old textbook. We must engage with it and let it affect us deeply. It's right to cry sometimes when we read the Bible. And when the Psalms tell us to shout for joy, maybe we should do that too!

DO IT YOURSELF

The prophet Jeremiah uses the image of water in many different ways. What sense is being conveyed by these different metaphors?

Jeremiah 2 v 13, 18:

Jeremiah 6 v 7:

Jeremiah 9 v 1:

Jeremiah 17 v 7–8:

Jeremiah 31 v 9:

Look at the four incidents recorded in **Mark 4 v 35 – 5 v 43**. How does Mark's use of detail help us to feel the extent of human helplessness before Jesus steps in?

Read **1 Samuel chapter 1**. How does the writer enable us to identify with Hannah's situation so that we're genuinely relieved and delighted when God intervenes?

Ideas taken from Dig Deeper by Nigel Beynon and Andrew Sach. Published by IVP and available from thegoodbook.co.uk

63 | 1 SAMUEL: Long live the king!

The story so far: Samuel anointed David as God's king. David killed Goliath. King Saul was jealous of David and tried to murder David. David is now on the run from Saul the slaughterer.

You might think with all this intrigue and slaughter that God would change His mind about letting Israel have a king. But no, God's plans to give His people their land and free them from all their enemies can't be stopped.

👁 Read 1 Samuel 23 v 1–5

ENGAGE YOUR BRAIN

▶ *What does this short episode seem to have to do with the whole David–Saul story?*

God's people are once again under threat from their old enemies, the Philistines. And just as God used David (His chosen king) to rescue them from the Philistines — and giant Goliath — last time, He does so again.

▶ *What are David's followers worried about? (v3)*

▶ *Seem reasonable?*

▶ *But what does God say? (v4)*

▶ *What does God's king accomplish? (v5)*

As God's chosen king, David points us to Jesus, a far greater King who dealt with far greater enemies.

PRAY ABOUT IT

Thank God that when you were helpless in your sin and facing His anger, He sent Jesus to die for you, and set you free. Use **Ephesians 2 v 1–10** to help you pray.

THE BOTTOM LINE

God's King rescues us from our enemies

→ TAKE IT FURTHER

Grab more on page 121.

64 A close call

More cat and mouse games now as Saul appears to be closing in on David. (Helpful info: The ephod that the escaping priest Abiathar brings with him was a God-given way of consulting God about yes/no type decisions.)

👁 Read 1 Samuel 23 v 6–12

ENGAGE YOUR BRAIN

▷ Why does Saul think he can trap David at Keilah? (v7)

▷ How will the people of Keilah treat David after he rescued them? (v12)

Huh! Not much gratitude for vanquishing the Philistines. But stop a minute — how much gratitude do we show God for all that He's done for us? Take time to read and pray about **Romans 12 v 1–2**.

👁 Read verses 13–26

▷ How sticky is the situation for David? (v13)

▷ But why is David safe? (v14)

▷ How does Jonathan encourage David?

▷ Who rats on David? (v19)

▷ How close does Saul get? (v26)

▷ How does God control outside events to rescue David in the nick of time?

God is in control of everything and yet He still cares for individuals. Wow.

PRAY ABOUT IT

Psalm 54 is another example of David turning his troubles into a psalm. Can you see how it links to the story you've just read about? Can you use it to shape your own prayers today?

THE BOTTOM LINE

God cares and God is in control.

→ TAKE IT FURTHER

More stuff on page 121.

65 | Hide and sneak

Yesterday we saw David saved in the nick of time. But Saul isn't giving up his manhunt any time soon. After dealing with the Philistine threat, he takes a hit squad to Engedi where David is hiding out...

Read 1 Samuel 24 v 1–7

ENGAGE YOUR BRAIN

▶ How does Saul unwittingly put himself in danger? (v3)

▶ How do David's men interpret this event? (v4)

▶ Do you think their advice is good?

▶ What does David do? (v4)

▶ Why does he change his mind? (v5–6)

David had good reason for attacking Saul while he had the chance but was content to leave things in God's hands.

GET ON WITH IT

Sometimes other people seem to give us good advice. The only way to check if it really is good advice is to see if it matches up with God's word. Get to know the Bible and let God be your adviser.

PRAY ABOUT IT

Do you find it hard to leave things to God when you have a (reasonable) grudge against someone else?

Romans 12 v 18–19 says: "If it is possible, as far as it depends on you, live at peace with everyone. Do not take revenge, my friends, but leave room for God's wrath, for it is written: 'It is mine to avenge; I will repay,' says the Lord."

Will you leave whatever is bothering you in God's hands today? Talk to Him about it now.

→ TAKE IT FURTHER

Sneak along to page 121.

66 | Rave from the cave

What will happen next? Will David simply let Saul get away? What will happen when Saul discovers he's missing part of his cloak?

👁 Read 1 Samuel 24 v 8–15

ENGAGE YOUR BRAIN

▶ *How does David address Saul? (v8, v11, v14)*

▶ *What does this demonstrate?*

▶ *How does David describe himself? (v14)*

▶ *What does this show about him?*

▶ *What does David say about God? (v10, v12, v15)*

Despite everything that has happened between them, David still treats Saul with all the respect due to his position as king. He publicly leaves the conflict between them for God to deal with and seeks reconciliation. This isn't the way we would expect him to act! God changes people!

PRAY ABOUT IT

Can you think back to a situation where it would have been easy to lose your temper or say something hurtful but God stopped you from doing it and helped you to forgive? Thank Him for His work in your heart.

If you can't (and even if you can!), ask Him to work in you through His Spirit today so that you can please Him.

👁 Read 1 Samuel 24 v 16–22

▶ *How does Saul respond to David's revelation? (v16)*

▶ *What does he recognise? (v17–20)*

▶ *What does he ask of David?*

▶ *Does David trust Saul despite all of this? (v22)*

Being a Christian doesn't mean we should be naive doormats. David knew that Saul had gone back on his promises before and was wise to stay out of his way. Jesus commands his disciples to be as wise as serpents but as innocent as doves. One church leader put it like this: we should be unshockable because we know how sinful people are, while fleeing the temptation to sin ourselves.

➔ TAKE IT FURTHER

Try page 122.

67 | Ab's fab

Does it ever take you a while to learn the same old lesson? You think you've got it sorted and then you forget it again — doh!

Read 1 Samuel 25 v 1–35

ENGAGE YOUR BRAIN

- ▶ What have David and his men done for Nabal? (v7)
- ▶ What does he ask in return? (v8)
- ▶ Can Nabal afford to do this? (v2)
- ▶ How does Nabal respond to David's polite request? (v10–11)
- ▶ How does David react? (v13, v21–22)

David is understandably annoyed, but things were heading for a nasty bloodbath were it not for the intervention of the lovely Abigail.

- ▶ What does Abigail discover? (v14–17)
- ▶ What does she do? (v18–19)
- ▶ How does she behave towards David? (v23–24)
- ▶ How is that different to Nabal?
- ▶ What does she remind David about? (v26, v28, v30–31)
- ▶ Who had sent her? (v32)

Phew! Abigail averts disaster in the nick of time — making peace, generously providing what David's men were owed and reminding David that God was in charge.

GET ON WITH IT

Are you a good Christian friend? Do you speak out when your brothers and sisters are about to do something foolish? Ask God for the grace to be a peacemaker and to remind other Christians about God's promises when they are about to make a mistake.

PRAY ABOUT IT

People need to be at peace with God. Pray for those you know who are living as God's enemies; that He would help you to share with them the peace that Jesus won for them.

THE BOTTOM LINE

Blessed be the peacemakers.

→ TAKE IT FURTHER

More fabulous Abigail on page 122.

68 | Fool's fate

Nabal means "fool" and we've seen him behaving pretty foolishly so far in chapter 25. And his next bit of behaviour tops it off.

👁 Read 1 Samuel 25 v 36–44

ENGAGE YOUR BRAIN

▶ What do we already know about Nabal from v11 and v17?

▶ What else do we discover about him in v36?

Grumpy, tight-fisted, incredibly arrogant (holds a feast as if he's a king, when he's rejected God's true king, David) and blind drunk. Foolish.

TALK IT OVER

Psalm 14 v 1 famously tells us: "The fool says in his heart, 'There is no God'". Chat to a Christian friend or youth group leader about why most foolish or evil behaviour can be traced back to this attitude.

▶ What is God's verdict on Nabal? (v38)

▶ How does David interpret what has happened? (v39)

▶ What is Abigail's happy ending?

Abigail is certainly better off with David. But notice that despite this "happy ending" David's first wife has been given to another man (v44) and, by marrying multiple times, David is not sticking to the Genesis chapter 2 blueprint. Trouble lies ahead and we're reminded that David is not the perfect king we need.

PRAY ABOUT IT

Thank God for Jesus, our perfect King. Pray for those who are foolishly rejecting Him, that they would repent before it is too late. Pray for people you know by name.

THE BOTTOM LINE

It is terminally foolish to reject God's King. It results in eternal death.

→ TAKE IT FURTHER

More foolish behaviour on page 122.

69 More sneaking around

Those pesky Ziphites again! Off they go to Saul with the latest info on where David is hiding. But God is still with David.

👁 Read 1 Samuel 26 v 1–25

ENGAGE YOUR BRAIN

▷ *Has Saul really given up pursuing David? (v2)*

▷ *What does David decide to do? (v6)*

▷ *What advice does Abishai give David? (v8) Sound familiar?*

▷ *And David's response? (v9)*

▷ *What does David again recognise about God's ways? (v10–11)*

God has really drummed this message into David. God is the king-maker and He calls the shots. Notice how God controls events to teach David this truth (see v12).

▷ *What does Saul learn once again? (v21)*

▷ *What is David's concern in all of this conflict? (v18–20)*

▷ *Does David come back as Saul asks him? (v21, v25)*

▷ *Why not? Is he right?*

David only wants to please the Lord. He wants to live in Israel, the land God gave to His people and where He promised to dwell with them. Which makes his next move rather strange... more on that tomorrow.

PRAY ABOUT IT

Thank God that you cannot be sent anywhere or go anywhere where He's not there. Read Psalm 139 and use it to help you talk to Him.

THE BOTTOM LINE

God is with us anywhere and everywhere.

TAKE IT FURTHER

Sneak over to page 122.

70 | Feelings and faithfulness

Poor David — you can understand why he was starting to despair of ever sorting things out with Saul. But what does he decide to do next? Hmmm...

Read 1 Samuel 27 v 1–12

ENGAGE YOUR BRAIN

▷ *How does David feel? (v1)*

▷ *Is he right? Why do you think he's thinking this way?*

GET ON WITH IT

The same David who had such faith in God's word back in chapter 26, seems to have given into the pressure in chapter 27. However much we know truths about God in our heads, sometimes our hearts let us down. We feel as if God doesn't care or as if He can't change things.

Dr Martyn Lloyd-Jones said in this type of situation we need to stop listening to ourselves (our worries and moans) and start "preaching to ourselves" — telling and reminding ourselves of all that God has done in the past and all that He has faithfully promised to do in the future. Try it now!

PRAY ABOUT IT

Now ask God to help you remember all of that!

▷ *Where does David go? (v2) Again?!*

▷ *Does his plan seem to be working? (v4)*

▷ *What does David do once he gets to the land of the Philistines? (v8–11)*

▷ *Why doesn't Achish suspect him? (v12)*

Sneaky! He might have left God's land but David's still at work disposing of Israel's enemies.

THE BOTTOM LINE

God is faithful, no matter how you feel.

→ TAKE IT FURTHER

A top tip on page 122.

71 | Saul summons Samuel's spirit

David is hanging out in the middle of his enemies, while his father-in-law Saul faces the violent anger of those same enemies. It's a bit of a cliffhanger — what will happen to each of them?

👁 Read 1 Samuel 28 v 1–3

ENGAGE YOUR BRAIN

▶ *What situation does David find himself in? (v1)*

▶ *Why is his answer sneaky but clever? (v2)*

▶ *What does the flashback in v3 remind us has happened?*

Saul appears to be doing the right thing here. God's law stated that witchcraft and fortune-telling was a definite no-no for the people of God. It was trusting in powers other than the Lord.

👁 Read verses 4–14

▶ *How does Saul respond to the Philistine threat? (v5)*

▶ *What is even worse than the threat of invasion? (v6)*

▶ *What bad choice does Saul make? (v7)*

▶ *What's wrong with Saul's oath? (v10)*

👁 Read verses 15–25

▶ *God's message to Saul remains the same — what does Samuel remind Saul? (v16–19)*

▶ *Why is there a certain logic about Saul's actions in v15 and God's response in v18?*

Part of the tragedy of God's judgment is that it is so totally fair. Saul didn't listen to God, so God won't listen to him. If we reject God, why should He then accept us? But the big picture we need to understand about what the Bible calls "hell" is that it isn't just the absence of God but His hostility and anger against His enemies (v16).

PRAY ABOUT IT

Saul faced the real hell of being abandoned by God. Pray now for those you know who are rejecting Him, that they would turn to Him.

THE BOTTOM LINE

Being without God is hell.

→ TAKE IT FURTHER

Spirit yourself over to page 122.

72 Trapped again?

Things aren't looking good for Saul, but what about David? Will he really join the Philistines in attacking Saul and Israel???

👁 **Read 1 Samuel 29 v 1–11**

▶ What is the dilemma David finds himself with? (v1–2)

▶ How does God get him out of it? (v3–4)

▶ What are the Philistine commanders worried about? (v4)

▶ Why have they good reason to be nervous of David? (v5)

▶ How does Achish see David? How does he describe David? (v6)

▶ Is he right to do so?

We know that the Philistine commanders are right to be suspicious of David's motives, but, somewhat naively, Achish has every confidence in David — see how God manages to get David out of fighting his own people but with no loss of honour or danger to his life (v10). An amazing rescue.

▶ What about Saul? Will he be rescued? What do you think?

▶ How does this chapter ominously end with a cliffhanger? (v11)

It's more than a little ironic that the king who doesn't trust David, (Saul), has every reason to, while the king who trusts him completely, (Achish), really shouldn't!

PRAY ABOUT IT
Thank God for Jesus: totally trustworthy and a wise and perfect King.

THE BOTTOM LINE
God is in control of everything.

→ **TAKE IT FURTHER**
Avoid the traps as you go to page 122.

73 Return to tragedy

It looks as if David's had a lucky escape, but there's trouble waiting for him at home...

Read 1 Samuel 30 v 1–2

▶ What has happened in David's absence? (v1–2)

▶ Why are these Amalekites still around to make trouble (look back to chapter 28 v 18)?

Saul's disobedience has far-reaching consequences and now David and his followers are suffering because of it.

Read verses 3–8

▶ How do David and his men react? (v4)

▶ What personal loss has David suffered?

▶ What is the second reaction of David's men? (v6)

▶ How did David react differently? (v6)

▶ How does God encourage David? (v8)

Interestingly David has learned his lesson about taking personal revenge (remember Nabal?) and despite pretty strong provocation, turns first to God to determine his course of action.

PRAY ABOUT IT

Do you find it hard to think before you speak? Or to refrain from snapping at someone when you're feeling annoyed? Ask God to help you where you find it hard not just to respond according to your sinful nature. Ask for the fruit of His Spirit — love, joy, peace, patience, kindness, goodness, faithfulness, gentleness and self-control.

THE BOTTOM LINE

Let God determine your actions.

→ TAKE IT FURTHER

A little bit more on page 122.

74 | Rescue mission

God has given David and his men the go-ahead to rescue their wives, children and belongings, but that doesn't mean it's going to be easy. Still, God has guaranteed that they will overtake and rescue.

Read 1 Samuel 30 v 9–31

ENGAGE YOUR BRAIN

▶ What happens to the number of rescuers? (v9–10)

▶ How does God help them when they're struggling? (v11–16)

▶ How completely does David succeed in the rescue? (v17–20)

▶ What trial does he face afterwards? (v22)

▶ What does David recognise about God? (v23)

▶ How does he treat his men (all of them)? (v24)

▶ How does he treat his countrymen of Judah? (v26)

▶ What sort of king does this suggest he'll be?

GET ON WITH IT

Do you give all the glory to God when you succeed at something? When you do well in your studies, or at sport? When you do something kind or helpful? Don't forget Him today.

PRAY ABOUT IT

Thank God for rescuing you when you were a helpless prisoner to sin and death. Thank Him that His rescue is sure and certain.

THE BOTTOM LINE

God gets the glory, because God rescues.

➡ TAKE IT FURTHER

Go on a mission to page 123.

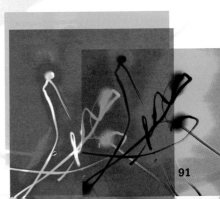

75 | End of part one

We've reached the end of 1 Samuel and the end of Saul too. A sad ending. Remember the Philistines? The enemies that God's people were supposed to defeat? The irony is that God now uses them to defeat His one-time king.

Read 1 Samuel 31 v 1–13

ENGAGE YOUR BRAIN

▶ *What happens to Jonathan? (v2)*

▶ *What about Saul? (v3)*

▶ *What do you think of Saul's request in v4? Brave? Kingly?*

▶ *What do you think he should have done?*

▶ *What's the ending for Israel? (v7)*

▶ *How do the Philistines insult Saul's memory and the people of Israel? (v9–10)*

▶ *Do you think God will let them continue thinking their idols and false gods helped them win?*

▶ *Why does this give us hope at the end of a bleak episode?*

▶ *What other small sign of compassion is there? (v11–13)*

Just as God promised, Saul is defeated. But remember what else God said would happen — there will be a new king, David. And more than that, God will never let His name be insulted. He may have used the Philistines to carry out His judgment on Saul, but they too will face His holy anger for their wicked deeds.

PRAY ABOUT IT

Remember the first line of the Lord's Prayer? "Our Father in heaven, hallowed be your name." Spend some time now asking God to act to keep the honour of His name... when people mock Him, deny His existence, do all kinds of evil in His name and persecute His people.

→ TAKE IT FURTHER

A happier ending on page 123?

76 | ISAIAH: God's perfect city

Let's turn our attention back to the gigantic book of Isaiah. There's a huge contrast between the disgusting way God's people have behaved and the perfect Servant God will send to give them a great future.

👁 Read Isaiah 50 v 1–3

God's people thought He had left them, like a husband divorcing his wife. God hadn't abandoned them — they had sinned against God so He rightly punished them, sending them into exile in Babylon. But, incredibly, He would bring them back. Nothing is impossible for Almighty God (v2–3).

👁 Read verses 4–9

ENGAGE YOUR BRAIN

🔹 *God's perfect Servant is speaking. How is He different from the Israelites? (v4–5)*

🔹 *How far was He prepared to go to obey God? (v6)*

🔹 *What helped Him cope with such violent opposition? (v7–9)*

Read verses 4–9 again, thinking about which parts specifically remind you of Jesus Christ.

👁 Read verses 10–11

🔹 *What's the first option for God's people? (v10)*

🔹 *What happens to those who choose to live for themselves instead of God? (v11)*

The way to make sure you treat God properly is to obey His Servant Jesus' word (v10); to do what He does, whatever you face in life (v4–9). God is more than strong enough to get us through. Relying on yourself (making your own "light", v11) brings God's punishment.

GET ON WITH IT

🔹 *From now on, will you complain at God, or trust His promises?*

🔹 *What do you need to change?*

PRAY ABOUT IT

Talk these issues over with God.

➔ TAKE IT FURTHER

More Servant stuff on page 123.

77 | Here's the good news

There's lots of bad news and good news in this part of Isaiah. The bad news: God's people were punished because of their sin. The good news: God's Servant would sort it all out.

👁 Read Isaiah 51 v 1–6

ENGAGE YOUR BRAIN

- Who is God speaking to? (v1)
- How would God transform His people and His city? (v3)
- Who is God's message of justice and salvation now for? (v4–6)

God's people would be transformed and their city (Zion/Jerusalem) will once again be beautiful and full of joy (v3). But God's message of justice now goes out beyond the Israelites to every nation of the world. Because of Jesus, everyone now has the chance to be part of God's people.

👁 Read verses 7–11

- Why don't God's people need to fear insults or attacks? (v7–8)
- What had God done in the past? (v9–10)
- So what will He do for His people in the future and how will they respond? (v11)

👁 Read verses 12–16

- Why is it dumb to fear people more than God? (v12–13)
- What did God promise His people who lived in fear? (v14)
- Why could they trust Him? (v15–16)
- What must they remember? (end of v16)

THINK IT OVER

- Who do you fear?
- What stops you from sharing the gospel more?
- How do these verses help your perspective?
- What will you do about it?

PRAY ABOUT IT

Talk to God about your fears and the things that stop you talking about Him. Ask Him to help you trust in His promises and fear only Him.

THE BOTTOM LINE

Fear God, not men.

→ TAKE IT FURTHER

More good news on page 123.

78   You snooze, you lose

"Wake up! Wake up!" shouts Isaiah. He challenges God's people to live the way they should as God's chosen people. Get up! Break free from those chains!

👁 Read Isaiah 51 v 17–23

ENGAGE YOUR BRAIN

▶ What had God's people, Israel, gone through? (v19)

▶ Who was punishing them? (v20)

▶ What happened to God's anger and punishment of His people? (v22–23)

Fear can paralyse us and make us useless. God's people were so fearful of their enemies, they stopped living God's way. But God took away His punishment and gave it to their enemies. So the people needed to "wake up!" and start serving God. For Christians, God sent Jesus to take away the punishment they deserve. So we should wake up and stop living in fear!

👁 Read Isaiah 52 v 1–10

▶ How does God say His people should live differently? (v1–2)

▶ What would happen to them? (v3–6)

▶ What's the great news? (v10)

▶ How should His people respond? (v8–9)

👁 Read verses 11–12

God's people must be awake and alert — ready for Him to rescue them from Babylon. And believers today should not snooze, living lazy lives, afraid of what people may think of them or do to them. Jesus has rescued us and one day will take us to live in God's new, perfect Jerusalem/Zion. He protects us, so we should live for Him with confidence.

PRAY ABOUT IT

Thank God for rescuing you and taking away the punishment you deserve. Pray that you will wake up and live for God, not in fear of others.

→ TAKE IT FURTHER

Wake up and turn to page 123.

79 | True beauty

We've already been introduced to the Servant who would rescue God's people from sin and its effects. Now we get a more specific description and it's surprisingly not very attractive.

👁 Read Isaiah 52 v 13–15

ENGAGE YOUR BRAIN

📘 Remember who this Servant is?

📘 What would happen to Him? (v13)

📘 Before that, how would people react to Him? (v14)

He would act wisely, yet go through terrible suffering that would leave Him disfigured. People would have nothing to do with Him, only later realising who He was. The "sprinkling" in v15 is about cleansing, making people clean enough to be in God's presence. This man, tortured and disfigured, would somehow bring people to God.

👁 Read Isaiah 53 v 1–3

📘 What would be surprising about God's chosen Rescuer? (v2)

📘 What else do we learn about Him in v3?

-
-
-
-

Despite many of the images of Jesus we see in paintings and movies, He was not stunningly attractive. And He would seem even less attractive when people hated and tortured Him. He would suffer greatly and many would turn away from Him, ashamed. Tomorrow we'll read why He went through such atrocious suffering.

PRAY ABOUT IT

Read today's verses about Jesus again and let your thoughts and feelings spill out to God.

➡ TAKE IT FURTHER

You've got more time to pray today, as there's no *Take it further*.

80 | A life for our lives

Isaiah is telling us more about the Servant —
Jesus Christ. This is vital, amazing, upsetting
stuff. Talk to God before you read this section,
so you're in the right frame of mind.

👁 Read Isaiah 53 v 4–6

ENGAGE YOUR BRAIN

▷ What did Jesus do about our sorrows and sins (iniquities)?

▷ What did He have to go through to rescue us? (v5)

▷ Did we deserve it? (v6)

👁 Read verses 7–9

▷ How did Jesus react to this horrific treatment? (v7)

▷ Did He deserve this? (v8–9)

▷ In your own words, how would you describe what Jesus went through for you?

👁 Read verses 10–12

▷ What did God willingly do? (v10)

▷ What would He then do? (v10)

▷ What would be the brilliant outcome? (v11)

▷ What did the future hold for Jesus? (v12)

▷ Why? (v12)

God crushed His own Son. But not because Jesus deserved it — it was the only way to pay for our disgusting sins and our rebellion against God. Jesus was prepared to go through terrible pain, suffering and loneliness for pathetic sinners like us! Incredible.

THINK IT OVER

It's the most outrageous swap: Jesus gets punished; sinful people get pardoned, forgiven. All of which begs a question: will you rely on yourself or on what Jesus has done for you?

PRAY ABOUT IT

Only you know exactly what you need to say to God right now. Make sure you do so.

→ TAKE IT FURTHER

Last minute substitution — page 123.

81 | Singing practice

Since God has taken action, through His Servant, to rescue His people from sin, the obvious response is… singing. Loud-voiced, full-hearted, belt-it-out singing. In chapter 54, we get reminders why.

Read Isaiah 54 v 1–8

ENGAGE YOUR BRAIN

- What does God call His people? (v1)
- Why should they sing? (v1–4)
- Why do they no longer need to live in fear? (v5–8)

Tents, descendants, a barren woman: it all reminds us of Abraham and Sarah. Just as God made it possible for Sarah to have a child and then a huge family, so He'd rebuild His people from just a small number in exile, to a huge, worldwide family of believers.

Read verses 9–17

- What did God promise after the flood in Noah's time? (v9)
- What did this mean for God's people? (v10)
- What did He promise about their future?
  v11–12:
  v13:

v14–15:
v17:

A new world of beauty and security. A city with God's presence and personal instruction. No fear there. And God's people get called servants (v17). The Servant (Jesus), by His great work, creates servants (Christians) who follow in His footsteps of suffering before glory. And it's they who'll benefit from all God's promises, which get fulfilled in the work of the Servant, Jesus. Awesome.

PRAY ABOUT IT

Read through this chapter's promises once more and then sing (or pray) your response to God. Ask Him to help you share your joy with others.

THE BOTTOM LINE

The future for God's people is worth singing about!

→ TAKE IT FURTHER

Another song on page 124.

82 | Feast your eyes on this

Over the last week, we've been reading about God's perfect Servant. Today, Isaiah rounds off the Servant section with a worldwide invitation.

👁 Read Isaiah 55 v 1–7

▣ *Who is God inviting to this amazing feast? (v4–5)*

▣ *How should they respond? (v1–2)*

▣ *What's the rich, satisfying food that's on offer? (v7)*

▣ *What will coming to the Lord involve? (v6–7)*

An amazing banquet has been laid on by God. No money is needed; it's already been paid for. The invited guests only need to accept and come. The "food" that's on offer is actually mercy and forgiveness. Jesus has already paid for it with His life. Best. Invitation. Ever.

👁 Read verses 8–13

▣ *What must people who accept God's invitation remember about Him? (v8–9)*

▣ *What are we told about what God says? (v10–11)*

▣ *What does the future hold for those who accept God's invitation? (v12–13)*

God's ways aren't like ours: just look at His extravagant, unlimited, outrageous generosity (v7).

Like rain, God's word comes from Him. And transforms stuff. His word is His chosen way of achieving His purposes. So His word to the world (v1) to "come to him" *will* be heard. And for those who respond, the future looks bright — a new world, with God's curse gone (v13). And a people from all over the globe, with Jesus leading them.

GET ON WITH IT

▣ *Do you need to obey v6?*

▣ *Who else do you need to tell about God's great invitation?*

PRAY ABOUT IT

Pick out the verses which really stand out to you and use them as you pray to the Lord.

➔ TAKE IT FURTHER

Feast on some more on page 124.

83 | Wait watching

Wait for it. From chapter 56 onwards, God's people are pictured as back from exile. But waiting. For God to bring about the final rescue from sin and launch His new world, as He'd promised.

👁 Read Isaiah 56 v 1–2

ENGAGE YOUR BRAIN

▶ *What should God's people do while they're waiting? (v1)*
▶ *What exactly are they waiting for? (v1)*
▶ *What shouldn't they do? (v2)*

God's people should stand together for justice and what is right — as a sign that God's reign of perfect justice and righteousness is just around the corner. For an explanation of the Sabbath stuff, go to *Take it further*.

GET ON WITH IT

▶ *What "right" things are you not doing at the moment?*
▶ *How can you "maintain justice"?*

👁 Read verses 3–8

Eunuchs were men who'd been castrated (probably in pagan rituals). "Foreigners" means non-Israelites. Both of these sections of society were considered outsiders by God's people.

▶ *But what shouldn't they say? (v3)*
▶ *What should outsiders do? (v6)*
▶ *What's the great news for outsiders who love God? (v5, v7)*

Being a Christian isn't about being in a club with people like yourself, where outsiders are excluded. God wants to bring many people into His kingdom and so we should show compassion to outsiders and welcome them in.

GET ON WITH IT

▶ *Which "weird" people will you show God's love to?*
▶ *How will you do it?*

PRAY ABOUT IT

Talk to God about anything He's challenged you about today.

➔ TAKE IT FURTHER

Sabbath stuff on page 124.

84 Beastly leaders

Again and again Isaiah shows the contrast between those who obey God and those who don't. The shock in this section is that "the wicked" were actually the leaders of God's people. What a mess.

👁 Read Isaiah 56 v 9 — 57 v 13

ENGAGE YOUR BRAIN

▷ How had Israel's leaders acted? (56 v 10–12)

▷ What did they do when good people were attacked? (57 v 1–2)

▷ What were they allowing to happen? (v5–6)

▷ What was God's message to them? (v12–13)

▷ But what about those who turned to God? (v13)

👁 Read Isaiah 57 v 14–21

▷ How are believers described? (v15)

▷ What's in store for them? (v15, v18–19)

▷ But what about anyone who rejects God? (v20–21)

God's people should be "contrite" — sorry for the way they've treated God — and ready to live His way now. God comforts us when we're overwhelmed by our sinfulness. He revives us, heals us, lifts our spirits until we can't help but praise Him.

God's people, (back from Babylon) were to wait for God's promised rescue. And live in the light of Him coming. Same for us. Waiting. Jesus has come and brought rescue. Now we're waiting for His return to wrap things up. So we should make sure we're living God's way as we wait.

PRAY ABOUT IT

Admit your failures to God and ask Him to comfort, heal and revive you.

THE BOTTOM LINE

There's no peace for the wicked, but God comforts those who turn to Him.

→ TAKE IT FURTHER

More bad shepherds on page 124.

85 | Home truths

God's people thought they were great and living His way and that they deserved great things from God. But the Lord had some home truths to put them straight.

👁 Read Isaiah 58 v 1–5

ENGAGE YOUR BRAIN

- ▷ *What did God's people seem to be like? (v2)*
- ▷ *But what was the truth? (v3–4)*

These people were highly religious. On the outside they looked super holy — keen to learn, going without food (fasting), wanting God to be close to them. But it was all a show. They didn't obey God; they fought and argued; they lived only for themselves. Their religion was just empty rituals.

👁 Read verses 6–12

- ▷ *What did God really want from His people? (v6–7)*
- ▷ *What will happen if God's people live like this?*
  v8:
  v9:
  v11:
  v12:
- ▷ *How can you fight injustice?*

- ▷ *Who's worse off than you who you could share stuff with?*
- ▷ *How can you make sure you get on better with your family?*

👁 Read verses 13–14

The way God's Old Testament people treated the Sabbath (day of rest) reflected their attitude to God. Would they organise their lives in order to respect it? For us today, the way we go on responding to Jesus (it's in Him that the Sabbath rest is fulfilled) reflects our attitude to God.

THINK IT OVER

- ▷ *What place does Jesus have in your life?*
- ▷ *How does the way you spend reveal your priorities?*

PRAY ABOUT IT

Talk to God openly about anything He's challenged you on today.

→ TAKE IT FURTHER

No *Take it further* today, so more time to think about today's challenges.

86 Payback time

Home truths. It can be hard to take when someone puts us straight about the way we've been behaving. Necessary but painful. God had some home truths for His people that would be hard to listen to.

👁 Read Isaiah 59 v 1–8

ENGAGE YOUR BRAIN

▶ *What was the terrible truth for God's people? (v2)*

▶ *What were they guilty of? (v7–8)*

The people of Judah had been moaning that God wasn't watching or listening to them. But they had been the ones to turn away from Him. Their violence, injustice and evil thoughts alienated them from God. That's what sin does — creates a barrier between us and God.

👁 Read verses 9–15

▶ *What is life like when you're separated from God? (v9–11, 14–15)*

▶ *What did these people do about their sinful situation? (v12–13)*

▶ *What sin do you need to admit to God right now?*

👁 Read verses 15–21

▶ *Amazingly, what did God do? (v16)*

▶ *How is the Lord described in v17?*

▶ *What will happen to His enemies and the enemies of His people? (v18)*

▶ *What about those who turn back to Him? (v20–21)*

PRAY ABOUT IT

Think about the way you've treated the Lord. Think about what He's done for you. Remembering that Jesus is coming back, what will you say to God right now?

→ TAKE IT FURTHER

Find a little more on page 125.

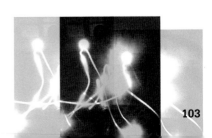

87 | Future perfect

It's time to take a great leap forwards: from the hideous reality of sin and judgment (chapter 59), to the awesome future (chapter 60) for those who rely on God and His Rescuer.

👁 Read verses 1–14

ENGAGE YOUR BRAIN

▷ What could happen to the darkness? (v1–2)

▷ How will this new dawn affect God's people? (v5)

▷ And what about the rest of the world? (v5–13)

▷ What will everyone have to realise? (v14)

A people transformed by God's personal presence. A group gathered from the around globe to glory in Israel's God. That's a huge turnaround for God's people who were living in exile. And it's a huge turnaround for believers — Jesus rescues us from the darkness of sin, bringing us into the light of God's glory.

👁 Read verses 15–22

▷ What's the big change for God's people? (v15)

▷ What will no longer exist for God's people in His city? (v18)

▷ And why no sun? (v19–20)

▷ What will be true for God's people? (v21–22)

What a future! Not just for God's faithful people from Judah, but for **all** believers. We'll live with Him in peace and perfection and sinlessness, in a city lit by God's glory. Astonishing! No one deserves this beautiful future, but God promises it to all who trust in Him.

GET ON WITH IT

▷ If this is the future for you, how should live now?

▷ So what will you do about it?

PRAY ABOUT IT

Read verses 15–21 again and praise God. Loads.

→ TAKE IT FURTHER

Back to the future on page 125.

88 | Fantastic future

Well done for getting this far in Isaiah. Stick at it, because the last few chapters are incredible. Yesterday we read about the perfect city where God's people are headed. Today we read about the perfect person.

👁 Read Isaiah 61 v 1–6

▶ *Who gave this incredible man his job? (v1)*

▶ *What was his great task? (v1)*

▶ *What was his message? (v2)*

▶ *What would be the result? (v3–6)*

In Luke chapter 4, Jesus makes it clear these verses are about Him. Let's just take in this awesome description of Him: Sent by God and given His Spirit; sent to preach good news to the poor; sent to mend hearts, rescue prisoners of sin; to comfort those who mourn; to punish God's enemies and raise up His chosen people. Magnificent.

👁 Read verses 7–11

▶ *What great swap would God bring about? (v7)*

▶ *Why? (v8)*

▶ *What would it lead to? (v8–9)*

▶ *So how should believers respond to God? (v10)*

▶ *Why? (v10–11)*

Here we see God's grace in action. We deserve shame and disgrace for our sinful lives, but believers have everlasting joy and inherit eternal life. They will be God's people for ever. The only right response to this undeserved, extravagant generosity is praise and worship.

PRAY ABOUT IT

So what are you waiting for? Verse by verse, use this remarkable chapter to praise and thank God for His perfect Son and His amazing grace.

→ TAKE IT FURTHER

More amazing truths on page 125.

89

Listen up!

God's speaking. So listen up. He's got great news for Jerusalem, and great news for us, too. So quickly pray right now, asking God to help you understand exactly what He wants to say to you today.

👁 Read Isaiah 62 v 1–7

ENGAGE YOUR BRAIN

ⓘ *What did the future hold for Jerusalem? (v1–2)*

ⓘ *How would the Lord transform His people? (3–5)*

ⓘ *What picture is used to describe God's relationship with His people?*

What an awesome prospect — God's people perfectly restored to an intimate relationship with Him. Everyone who longs for that will pray their socks off for it (v6–7).

👁 Read verses 8–12

ⓘ *What is God's irreversible promise to His people? (v8–9)*

ⓘ *Who are people waiting for? (v10–11)*

ⓘ *What great names will God's people be called? (v12)*

ⓘ *What's this tell us about them?*

God's people back then — and today too — were constantly attacked and faced tough times. But God has promised a day when they will no longer be exploited and persecuted. Instead, God will live among the people He's rescued for Himself, a people made fit for Him. A perfect future for God's people.

PRAY ABOUT IT

Like the watchmen of Jerusalem (v6–7), let this great news affect the way you pray. Keep thanking God for the perfect future that belongs to all who trust in Jesus the Saviour.

THE BOTTOM LINE

"They will be called the Holy People, the Redeemed of the Lord".

→ TAKE IT FURTHER

For the big picture, turn to page 125.

90 | Punishment and praise

We're still reading about the conquering hero who would rescue God's people and defeat their enemies for good. Today we'll see Him act in horrific vengeance and see Isaiah's surprising response.

👁 Read Isaiah 63 v 1–6

ᴅ *What did this conqueror do? (v3)*
ᴅ *Why? (v4–5)*

Finally, the tables are turned. This conquering hero is dishing out God's judgment: His personal, end-time punishment of all who oppose Him and His people. Not a pretty sight.

👁 Read verses 7–19

ᴅ *What had God done for the Israelites? (v8–9)*
ᴅ *But what happened? (v10)*
ᴅ *What did God's people remember about their past history? (v11–14)*
ᴅ *What did Isaiah want God to do in the current dark times? (v15–17)*

God piled goodness on His people, shared their crises even when they rejected Him, acted in mercy even when filled with anger. He rescued, provided, guided. Yet His people continued to reject Him and so they were being trampled by their enemies.

👁 Read Isaiah 64 v 1–12

ᴅ *What did Isaiah remember about God? (v4–5)*
ᴅ *Yet how are His people described? (v5–6)*
ᴅ *And how did God rightly respond? (v7)*
ᴅ *So what did Isaiah pray? (v9)*
ᴅ *Why? (v8, v10–11)*

God's people continued to sin, so God continued to punish them. Isaiah asked the Lord: "Where?" (63 v 15), "Why?" (63 v 17), "How?" (64 v 5). Isaiah was baffled and fearful, but still holding on to God's commitment to His people. Isaiah didn't fully understand what was going on, but knew God had rescued His people in the past and would do so again.

THE BOTTOM LINE

When you don't understand why bad stuff is happening, remember God is perfect and never leaves His people.

➔ TAKE IT FURTHER

A little bit more on page 125.

91 God answers

Yesterday Isaiah prayed for God's mercy on His people. He asked the question: would God continue to punish His people, without end? Today, God answers.

👁 Read Isaiah 65 v 1–7

ENGAGE YOUR BRAIN

▶ *How had God acted? (v1–2)*

▶ *How did the people respond? (v2–5)*

▶ *What would have to follow such despicable actions? (v6–7)*

👁 Read verses 8–16

▶ *What is God's incredible promise to His faithful people? (v8–10)*

▶ *What about those who continue to reject God? (v11–12)*

▶ *Why? (v12)*

▶ *List the end results for both sets of people (v13–16)...*
God's servants:

God's enemies:

👁 Read verses 17–25

▶ *When Jesus returns, what will change? (v17)*

▶ *What will this new city be like? (v18–19)*

▶ *How else will it be great?*
v21–22:
v23:
v24:
v25:

Mind-blowing stuff. This whole sinful world will be replaced with a new creation. Nothing harmful will be a part of it (v25) and believers will live in this paradise with their God.

PRAY ABOUT IT

Read through chapter 65 again and...
• say sorry for specific sins
• thank God for His perfect promises of a brilliant future for His people
• pray for people who reject Him.

→ TAKE IT FURTHER

No *Take it further* today.

92 | God's perfect city

Through Isaiah, God's been talking about judgment and rescue. As we reach the end of this huge book, it's time to double-check: who will share in God's new world?

👁 Read Isaiah 66 v 1–6

▣ *Why is it so amazing that God will live among His people? (v1–2)*

▣ *Who will He live with? (v2)*

▣ *What does He think of "religion" that doesn't involve actually living for Him? (v3)*

▣ *What will happen to those who live only for themselves? (v4)*

👁 Read verses 7–17

A big boost for Isaiah's listeners who trusted God's word: out of His judgment on Israel, a new people would suddenly be born (v7–8). God would do it (v9). This is the church of God — believers.

▣ *What would this new people enjoy? (v11–13)*

▣ *What must everyone remember? (v14–17)*

👁 Read verses 18–25

▣ *What amazing thing will God do? (v18)*

▣ *How would He do it? (v19–20)*

▣ *What will be true for this rescued people? (v22–23)*

▣ *What would be a reminder of God's mercy to them? (v24)*

That's it! Isaiah's in the bag. What a marathon. Well done! And what a vision: the new Jerusalem, brought about by God's chosen one: the King who suffered and died for His people and will return as Judge. King Jesus.

PRAY ABOUT IT

Think what Isaiah has taught you about yourself and about King Jesus. Talk to God about it.

→ TAKE IT FURTHER

There's nothing left to say about Isaiah, so thank God for all you've learned. Ask Him to help you live His way as you wait for the King's return.

TAKE IT FURTHER

If you want a little more at the end of each day's study, this is where you come. The TAKE IT FURTHER sections give you something extra. They look at some of the issues covered in the day's study, pose deeper questions, and point you to the big picture of the whole Bible.

RUTH
God's big love story

1 – WHO DO YOU THINK YOU ARE?
Read James 1 v 2–8

▷ *What can the testing of our faith produce?*

▷ *What do we need when we ask for help?*

Tough times are confusing. It's normal to ask why, and to struggle for answers. For sure, some suffering can be for a good reason, but at other times it seems pointless. The one thing we must do is remember that God is good. He is not and never can be the enemy of what's right (James 1 v 16–17).

Write the words "God is good. ALL the time." somewhere obvious. Make this a daily reminder of His changeless nature.

2 – CLINGING ON

As God's people, heading for eternal life, we know that all suffering will end… eventually. So we don't have to give up hope even when things seem super grim.

▷ *What good can pain do? (James 1 v 2–4)*

▷ *What fact about God must we cling to? (James 1 v 16–17)*

Dare to thank God that not everything in your life today is perfect.

3 – DON'T JUST SIT THERE!
Read Ruth 2 v 3

As Ruth continues her food-gathering mission, the narrator suggests she is not aware of the one who owns the field, nor that he's a relative. But it seems this is no coincidence — God is at work behind the scenes to bring them together!

▷ *What proportion of life's events are under God's control?*

Read Romans 8 v 28 and Ephesians 1 v 11

These verses express that God is sovereign, that is, He is directly in charge of everything that happens all over planet earth. This doesn't mean He takes our freedom away, but that ultimately, nothing can obstruct His good purposes.

Read James 5 v 10–11

ⓘ *What is the Bible's view of people who persevere?*

In a world that demands instant results, quitting is fashionable. But stickability is godly. If you're toughing it out through a testing time, remember you're not alone. Hold on. Ask the King of kindness to give you His strength for as long as it takes.

5 – COMFORT VS COMMITMENT

Read Mark 8 v 34–38

ⓘ *What actions lead to...*
  losing your life?
  forfeiting your soul?
  Jesus being ashamed?

Carrying your cross and dying might sound a bit extreme. But as Jesus makes clear, anything less is empty religion. The only type of faith worth having is wholehearted. To choose a safer option actually leaves us with nothing. The only sensible thing is to give everything to Him. Do you find this sort of challenge hard to hear? Find an older Christian you trust and ask them to help you go deeper as a disciple.

6 – NEW-LOOK LOVE

Boaz is the leading man in quite a love story. It's a foretaste of something even more moving.

Read 1 John 3 v 16–17

This kind of commitment is not just reserved for marriage.

ⓘ *Who defines love's real meaning?*
ⓘ *Who does God call us to love?*
ⓘ *What action proves our lack of love?*

Love is to be the trademark among Christians. And that means turning good intentions into action. What loveless moments do you need to confess? Ask the King of love for courage to live a laid-down life.

7 – THE COMEBACK KING

Read 1 Peter 1 v 18–19

ⓘ *In what way is Jesus different to silver and gold?*
ⓘ *What kind of lamb is He?*

See why this is significant in Exodus 12 v 1–14

The story of Israel's miraculous exodus from Egypt gives us the core meaning of redemption. As God's anger burned against Pharaoh and his people because of their stubborn resistance, only those households marked with the lamb's blood were saved from death. The sacrifice of the lamb was the key to Israel's freedom. Now Jesus is our Passover lamb, we too are redeemed by putting our faith in His sacrifice. Make this a day to live like the rescued. Walk in freedom and worship your Redeemer!

8 – HISTORY MAKERS

Ruth found taking refuge under the "wings" of the God of Israel (2 v 12) worked. It was almost as if He was actively encouraging foreigners to make themselves at home....

Read Isaiah 49 v 5–6
▷ *What is the small thing that the servant is given to do?*
▷ *What is the bigger thing?*
If it was ever in doubt, Isaiah sees clearly that God's ultimate plan is not just for one nation. It's for every nation — to the ends of the earth! And this was in God's mind from the beginning.

Read Genesis 12 v 3
▷ *Which people would inherit a blessing through Abraham?*
Jesus is for every kind of person. How can you deliberately reach out beyond your "own kind" today?

TITUS
Getting it right

9 – HI, TITUS!
Read verse 2 again
then Philippians 1 v 6
God doesn't lie. Ever. When He promises something, He always delivers.
▷ *How certain can you be that you have eternal life?*
▷ *Why?*
Need more evidence? See **John 5 v 24**.

10 – LEAD BY EXAMPLE
Read 1 Timothy 3 v 1–7
▷ *What similarities are there with the description in Titus?*
▷ *Any differences?*

▷ *Why is it important for a church leader to have a good reputation outside of the church? (v7)*
Paul says that aspiring to leadership and responsibility is a "noble task" to aim for (v1). Should you be considering some form of Christian leadership?

11 – DISHONEST DECEIVERS
Paul opposed teachers who said Christians had to keep Jewish food laws and get circumcised. He insisted we're put right with God by trusting in Jesus, not by keeping the Jewish law. The problem with trying to get right with God by keeping the Old Testament law is that we have to keep all of it. And no one can possibly do that.

Read Galatians 3 v 10–14
▷ *Why can't anyone be put right with God by keeping the law?*
▷ *Why does Paul say we're put right with God by trusting Jesus?*

12 – EQUAL TO THE TASK
Phrases like "be busy at home" and "be subject to their husbands" can really upset some Christians. John Stott explains these verses helpfully:

"This "subjection" contains no inferiority and no demand for obedience, rather a recognition that, within the equal value of the sexes, God has created an order which includes a masculine "headship", not of authority ... but of responsibility and loving care. And one of the reasons

the younger women are to be encouraged to comply with this teaching is "so that no one will malign the word of God" (v5). Christian marriages and Christians homes, which exhibit a combination of sexual equality and complementarity, beautifully commend the gospel; those which fall short of this ideal bring the gospel into disrepute."

13 – LIFE LESSONS
Read Colossians 3 v 18 – 4 v 1

▶ *At home, what's the marriage relationship to be like?*

▶ *At home, how much should we obey our parents? (v20)*

▶ *Why?*

▶ *In work (of whatever kind), how do the principles of v22–25 apply to us?*

▶ *Do you work harder when someone's watching or you're being paid for it, or it's something you like?*

▶ *What does v23 say about this?*

14 – HEART OF THE MESSAGE
**Read verse 14 again
and then Ezekiel 37 v 23**

By His death and resurrection, Jesus purified for Himself a people of His own. God took people who were morally dirty, who disobeyed God — and cleaned them up. Just as Israel was God's special people before Christ came, now Christians are God's special people.

Read Titus 2 v 11–12 again

▶ *What 2 things does God's grace do?*

It doesn't just save us once off and then

we carry on as before. No, it trains us to live differently.

▶ *How do you think this might happen?*

Tired of trying to live for Jesus but failing? God offers both constant forgiveness and help to keep going.

▶ *What do you need to ask God for?*

▶ *How does it help to look back (v11, v14) and forward (v13)?*

15 – GET ON WITH IT!
Read Romans 13 v 1–7

▶ *Why should we obey people with authority over us?*

v1:

v3:

v5:

▶ *Who are we really rebelling against if we don't obey laws and those in authority? (v2)*

▶ *What responsibilities do governments have? (v4)*

Our duty is to obey the authorities over us. And their job is to obey God, by promoting good and pounding evil. Think of people in authority over you and use these verses to help you pray for them.

16 –BATH TIME
**Read verse 5 again
and then John 3 v 5–8**

▶ *How do these verses fill out the description of the new birth we get?*

The idea of being "born in water" is the same as Paul's idea of "washing" (Titus 3 v 5) — being cleansed of our guilt by

Jesus' death for us. The idea of being "born of the spirit" is the same as Paul's idea of rebirth and renewal in Titus. The Holy Spirit makes us alive to God when we come to believe in Jesus and His death for us. That's what being born again means.

17 – ARGU-MENTAL
Read 1 Timothy 1 v 3–7

Verse 4 probably refers to writings that were popular between Old and New Testament times. Also, it seems that people were using family trees (genealogies) to try to prove their ancestry — as if that made them more "in" with God. Crazy.

▶ *What was the effect of these things on the church? (v4, v6, v7)*

▶ *Yet what's the only way to know God? (v4)*

▶ *And what should that result in? (v5)*

18 – FOND FAREWELL
Note down five things:

1. One thing you've found encouraging from the book of Titus.
2. One verse you want to remember.
3. One thing you want to pray about.
4. Summarise from Titus how Christians should relate to the non-Christian world.
5. How will you make progress with this?

19 – JUDGE DREAD
Read Proverbs 31 v 8–9

▶ *How can you do that this week?*

1 SAMUEL
Long live the king!

20 – A NEW KING
Read verse 7 again

God's choice of king here is unlikely.

▶ *How is Jesus an unlikely king? Think about His birth, His parents, and His background.*

▶ *How is He perfectly qualified?*

Check out Philippians 2 v 6–11

21 – SAUL GONE WRONG
Take a look at John 3 v 16–19

▶ *What is the consequence of rejecting God?*

▶ *What does God want and not want?*

▶ *What is the outcome if we believe in Jesus?*

▶ *How could you use John 3 v 16 to explain to your friends what Jesus is offering?*

22 – GIGANTIC BATTLE
Take another look at verses 8–9

Goliath is essentially proposing that he and A.N.Other Israelite act as substitutes for the whole nation. Can you think of another occasion when an individual stood in for many?

Check out Romans 5 v 6–8 and 12–19

23 – STONE DEAD
Goliath seemed like a pretty powerful and terrifying enemy, while David looked small and weak. Jesus looked pretty small and weak too as He died on the cross, but in trusting His Father, He defeated those

mighty enemies; sin and death.
See 1 Corinthians 1 v 18–25

God's people now enjoy the results of that victory as we accept Jesus' rescue: friendship with God; forgiveness; rescue from our greatest enemy, the devil; God's gift of life with Him forever. Take in the great list from **Ephesians 1 v 3–14**.

24 – FROM NICE TO NASTY
How will these passages help you to view your life?
Luke 12 v 4–5
Ephesians 2 v 10
Romans 8 v 28–39 — why not learn this by heart?

25 – FAMILY MISFORTUNE
God is always in control of events.
Read **Genesis 50 v 15–20** and
Acts 2 v 22–41 and ask yourself:
▶ *What did people try to do?*
▶ *What did God do?*

26 – FRIENDS AND ENEMIES
▶ *How does God show that He is behind David's preservation? (v18–24)*
▶ *How does this chapter make you feel about Saul?*
▶ *Pray for people you know who are pointlessly opposing God, that they would repent and that God would have mercy on them.*

27 – SPLITTING HEIRS
David keeps the promise he makes to Jonathan in v15 and v42.

Read 2 Samuel 9 v 1–13
▶ *Would you expect a descendant of Saul to be David's enemy?*
▶ *Does Mephibosheth have anything to offer David?*
▶ *How does David treat Mephibosheth?*
▶ *Can you see parallels with the way God's King, Jesus, treats us?*

28 – GOING CRAZY
David wrote a number of psalms about the troubles he experienced at this period of his life.
Look at Psalm 34
▶ *How does understanding these events help you gain more from this psalm?*
▶ *What does David do to encourage others to praise God? (v1)*
▶ *What do you think "boast in the Lord" (v2) means?*
▶ *When do you need to do that?*
▶ *How did David respond to the situation he was in? (v4)*
▶ *How did God respond to David? (v6–7)*
▶ *What's your first reaction in awkward situations? Why?*
▶ *How do we find out that God is good? (v8)*
▶ *What will be the result? (v9–10)*
▶ *Verses 11–14 explain how to live fearing God. Do v13–14 characterise your behaviour?*
▶ *How does God treat the righteous — those who fear God? (v15, v17–20)*
▶ *And the wicked? (v16, v21)*

29 – OUTLAW AND DISORDER

Here's another one of David's autobiographical psalms!

Look at Psalm 52

ⓘ *How does understanding these events help you gain more from this psalm?*

30 – KING OF EVERYTHING

Read verses 9–10
and then Judges 4 v 1–24

ⓘ *What do you learn about God from this story?*

Read Psalm 83 v 11–12
then Judges 7 v 1 – 8 v 21

What do you learn from this story...
– about God?
– about serving Him?
– about His enemies?

ISAIAH
God's perfect city

31 – GOD'S HIGHWAY

Read verse 3 again
and then Mark 1 v 1–8

In the Old Testament, God promised to send His King to rescue His people. Now, after 400 years without a word from God, His spokesman, John the Baptist, has a message. Notice what it is? (v7) Now wonder there was total, national mayhem (v5).

ⓘ *How did John prepare the people for Jesus?*

John could only do something external — dunk them in water.

ⓘ *How would Jesus' work be far more significant, and why? (v8)*

32 – FADE AWAY

Verses 1–11 set us up for the themes of chapters 40–55.

God would bring exiles home: check out
Isaiah 48 v 20–21

And He's also bringing about a far greater rescue for them and for the world:
Isaiah 42 v 1–4; 49 v 1 & 6; 55 v 1–13
How? Through a sin-bearing servant, as we'll soon see.

33 – NO COMPARISON

Here's how a guy called Barry Webb sums up v12–26:

"Isaiah paints a breathtaking picture of God ... He created the universe as effortlessly as a skilled craftsman constructing a model on his workbench (v12). He is infinitely wise (v13–14), totally sovereign (v15, v17), worthy of more worship than we could ever give Him (v16), incomparable (v18–20) and enthroned above the circle of the earth (v22–24). "Lift up your eyes," says Isaiah, "and see who it is who has given you His word."

ⓘ *How will you respond to this God?*

34 – COURTROOM DRAMA

Read verses 2 and 25

This is talking about Cyrus, the Persian ruler who whupped Babylon and let the exiles from Judah return to Jerusalem.

Cyrus was no worshipper of God, but he was aware of God and referred to Him (Ezra 1 v 1–4). More on Cyrus later!

35 – GOD'S SERVANT
Read Matthew 12 v 14–21

▷ *What do Jesus' actions (v15) tell us about Him? (v17)*

People wrongly expected a hard, defeat-the-Romans type Messiah. Instead, Jesus came just as the Old Testament said He would.

▷ *What marked Jesus out? (v18–21)*
▷ *What had He come to do?*

This is Matthew's big point. Jesus' mission is not limited; it's to the "nations" — the world (v21). To those who would receive Him, unlike most of the Pharisees and Jews back then.

36 – SONGS AND WRONGS
Read verse 20 again

Israel's sin was worse because they should have known better. The word of God was revealed to them but they ignored it. That's a warning for anyone who has received good Bible teaching for months or years.

▷ *Are you living out what you've learned?*
▷ *How should we measure progress in our lives? (Isaiah 43 v 7, 21)*

37 – THE ONE AND ONLY
Today we read about God's comfort for His terrified people. Psalm 3 also has comfort in scary circumstances. It was written by David when he was on the run from Absalom, his son. David had made a strategic withdrawal from Jerusalem, crossed rivers and mountains and gone for miles. This prayer follows his first night on the run. Notice how God gave him sleep and calm.

Read Psalm 3

What made David calm? Despite his situation, he realised:

1. God was sufficient even for his crisis moment (v1–3).
2. Prayer brought peace and real assurance about the future (v4–8).

First, David turned to God, and then in answer to prayer, received rest from God. Then he could go forward with God into the intimidating, unknown future.

38 – WHAT'S IN A NAME?
Read Isaiah 43 v 22–25

Amazingly, the God who is wearied by our heavy sins is the God who blots them out and refreshes us.

▷ *Do you need to pause and take this in properly?*

39 – IDOL TALK
More wise words from Barry Webb on Isaiah: *"Idolatry is the worst sin of all because it moves God to the periphery of our lives and puts something else in His place. It gives something else the glory which should be God's alone. Chameleon-like, it constantly disguises itself so that we are scarcely aware of its presence, even when we are most in the grip of it.>*

Greed, Paul tells us, is idolatry, because it turns us away from God towards things, and makes the pursuit of them the passion of our lives [see Colossians 3 v 5]. The modern world is no less given over to idolatry than the ancient one."

41 – POETIC TRUTH

This poem is a great vision of a worldwide people of God. Remember what it is we're saved from? God's anger at our sin that must end in judgment and punishment. Salvation is for the world, but not all will be saved (v24–25).

🄳 *How will this change your thinking and prayers about family and friends who don't know this yet?*

43 – FOOLS FREED

Read verses 1–2 again

Notice the contrast between Israel's calling and the response they made to God. A proud claim (v2a), but no reality.

🄳 *Does this ring true for you too?*

🄳 *Does your life match up to what you claim about yourself and your faith?*

44 – LIGHT RELIEF

Read verse 8 again

What does it mean that Jesus would be a "covenant for the people"? Well, God is saying that it's now *in him* (Jesus) that all the benefits promised throughout the Bible are found. For example...

Read Ephesians 1 v 1–14

🄳 *List all the "in him" blessings:*

🄳 *Do you realise all that you've got*

in Christ?

45 – FORGIVEN, NOT FORGOTTEN

🄳 *Do you ever say or think stuff like verse 14?*

🄳 *Yet what does God promise His people?*

v14–16:

v17–20:

v21–23:

v24–26:

🄳 *Why should we trust God's promises above our feelings?*

ACTS
Under pressure

46 – CHRISTIAN SENSE

Paul is putting into action what Jesus had encouraged His followers to do.

Read Mark 8 v 31–38

Pick out the challenging ways Jesus said His followers should live.

🄳 *How have we seen Paul living these things out, both in today's passage and more generally in Acts?*

47 – BEND OVER BACKWARDS

Read Acts 21 v 17–19

🄳 *What does Paul recognise about all that's happened among the Gentiles (non-Jews) he's told the gospel to?*

It's a great reminder of Paul's humility; and a great encouragement to us. Evangelism is God's work, not ours; but God gives us the privilege of being part of spreading the message of Jesus. A great reason to get on with telling those around us about Jesus; and a great reminder to give praise to God whenever somebody becomes one of His people!

48 – BUT SERIOUSLY
Read Acts 22 v 4–9

▷ *Who was Paul persecuting? (v4)*

▷ *Who did Jesus say Paul was really persecuting? (v7-8)*

▷ *What does this tell us about Jesus' view of His relationship with His people?*

49 – SO MANY VOICES
The Sadducees' refusal to believe in life after death didn't just make them opponents of Paul; it also saw them opposing Jesus.

Check out Mark 12 v 18–27

▷ *What is the Sadducees' cunning objection to the existence of eternal life? (v20–23)*

▷ *What points does Jesus make in answering? (v25–27)*

▷ *What's the Sadducees' big problem that means they're "badly mistaken"? (v24)*

50 – WE'LL KILL HIM!
God's people have often found themselves surrounded by those who want to harm them or use them.

Read Psalm 3, 4 or 12 (or all three!)

These were written by King David, 1,000 years before Paul was alive.

▷ *How does knowing God encourage*

David when life is hard?

51 – COURT-ING CONTROVERSY
It's amazing Paul's enemies accuse Paul of "stirring up riots among the Jews all over the world" (v5). In fact it's the Jews who stirred up riots because they rejected Paul's message about Jesus (have a look at Acts 14 v 4–7, 19–20; 16 v 19–24; 17 v 5–8). All Paul was doing was preaching about Christ, not provoking riots!

▷ *What does this remind us about the reception the gospel message often receives?*

52 – WHEN BEING OFFENSIVE IS GOOD
Read Acts 25 v 10–12

As a Roman citizen on trial for his life, Paul had the right to be tried by the emperor, or "Caesar". Rather than be killed by the Jews on the way to Jerusalem, Paul asks to stand before Caesar in Rome (v11). He's willing to die for his faith in Christ; but he's not willing to die for the made-up accusations the Jewish leaders have brought against him (v10–12).

It's worth noticing that when he can, Paul uses his status as a Roman citizen to protect himself. But he's not doing that so he can have an easier life: he's doing it so he can have more chances to tell others about Jesus.

▷ *How can you use any advantages and privileges you have for the same goal?*

53 – CHRISTIANITY ON TRIAL
Jesus told Paul: "it is hard to kick against

the goads" (v 14). The goads were a way of controlling an animal so it went where you wanted, and Jesus is pointing out to Paul how pointless it is to oppose Him. Paul seemed to have been doing very well persecuting Jesus' followers and shutting down His churches, but in fact Jesus was still alive, still in charge, and still able to bring people to see who He was.

Psalm 2 makes the same point about the patheticness of opposing Jesus, God's King. Read it now.

54 – RESPONSE TO A RESPONSE
**Check out Psalm 22
and/or Isaiah 52 v 13 – 53 v 12**
Both of these are prophecies, written centuries before Jesus lived on earth.
▶ *How are these prophets predicting, as Paul told Agrippa, what "would happen — that the Christ would suffer and … rise from the dead" (Acts 26 v 22–23)?*

55 – WHEN TIMES GET TOUGH
Check out some of God's amazing promises:
Romans 8 v 1, 8 v 11, 8 v 28, 8 v 38-39
Why not memorise some of these so you can remember and trust them when life is hard?

56 – PUT YOUR FEET UP?
Re-read Acts 27 v 33–37
▶ *Paul urges everyone to eat — what does he do before they start the meal?*
It's interesting that Paul does this on a ship

full of people who aren't Christians. Often Christians give thanks to God for their food when they're with other Christians — wouldn't it be a great witness to do it when you're with people who aren't trusting Christ?! You could do it quite quietly, without stopping everyone else, and so make clear to those around you that you thank God for everything, and that you take your faith seriously. You never know, it might prompt people to ask you some questions about your faith!

58 – DONE ROME-IN
Years before Paul got to Rome in person, he'd sent them a letter. We call it (yes, you've guessed it) "Romans".
Read Romans 1 v 11–17
▶ *Why did Paul long to see the Roman Christians? (v 11–12)*
▶ *How did Paul feel about the gospel, and why? (v 16–17)*
▶ *What does v 14–15 suggest we can expect to see Paul doing in Rome now that he's finally reached it?*

59 – THE END?
It's easy to think that when Paul told people about Jesus, loads and loads of them became Christians (unlike when we try!) But have a look at **Acts 28 v 24**, where Paul's talking to Jews… and **Acts 17 v 32–33**, where he's talking to non-Jews…
▶ *What kind of proportion of Paul's listeners become Christians on these two occasions?*
▶ *What does this remind us about*

evangelism?

▶ *How is this an encouragement to us to keep talking about Jesus to those around us?*

PSALMS

60 – LONGING FOR GOD

Read verse 9 again

"The shield" and "your anointed" both refer to the king of God's people (David and his successors). The writer wanted God to look favourably on His people and their king, and treat them well. The ultimate King is Jesus. We know God favours His people and looks after them because He sent Jesus to rescue them.

62 – SAVE DAVE

This psalm has the word "Lord" — ruler who's in charge; and "LORD" — the special family name for God, which showed He'd committed Himself to His people. Cool, eh?

Read verse 15 again

David knows his Scripture so well he quotes it (Exodus 34 v 6) And, although we're not told how and when God answered his prayer, we see David trusting in God, confident he'll be answered.

▶ *What challenge has this psalm brought for you?*

1 SAMUEL

63 – LONG LIVE THE KING!

Take some time to see how God's King, Jesus, deals with our enemies in **1 Corinthians 15 v 24–26 and v51–57.**

64 – A CLOSE CALL

Read Psalm 54

▶ *What three things did David ask God for? (v1–2)*

▶ *What sort of danger was he in? (v3)*

▶ *What is it about God that he appealed to? (v1)*

God's name (which reflects His character) and His power: David knew God is not only willing to save, but also able to. As in other psalms, the response in times of trouble is to pray. Have you learned this?

▶ *What did David stop to remember? (v4)*

▶ *Could you say this too?*

▶ *What truth about God was David certain of? (v5)*

▶ *What did David say he would do? (v6)*

▶ *And why? (v7)*

Geddit? David was so sure of God's goodness that he spoke in verse 7 as if God had rescued him already. Superb.

65 – HIDE AND SNEAK

1 Peter 2 v 18–25 has a lot to say about suffering unjustly. Read it now.

▶ *What is the situation being addressed in v18?*

▶ *What are Christians called to do? (v21)*

▶ *Why would this be hard?*

▶ *Whose example are they following?*
▶ *How would this help them (and us)?*
Someone once said the question to ask when we suffer is not: "Is it worth it?" but: "Is He worthy?"

66 – RAVE FROM THE CAVE
Take another look at verse 19
▶ *How does Jesus live up to and surpass His ancestor David in Romans 5 v 6–8?*

67 – AB'S FAB
▶ *What does Abigail recognise about God's promises? (v28–30)*
▶ *Are we as confident in what God has promised us?*
Remind yourself of Matthew 28 v 20, Romans 8 v 28–30 and Revelation 22 v 20

68 – FOOL'S FATE
Read the parable in Luke 12 v 13–21
▶ *How is the farmer like Nabal?*
▶ *How is he like people you know?*
▶ *What "barns" are we tempted to build in our lives?*
▶ *What is the most important thing in life?*

69 – MORE SNEAKING AROUND
How does God's presence with His people change through the Bible? Follow the trail...
**Genesis 3 v 8 , Exodus 13 v 21–22
Exodus 40 v 34–38 , 1 Kings 8 v 27
Matthew 1 v 23 & 28 v 20
John 14 v 16–17, Acts 2 v 1-4
and finally Revelation 21 v 3**

70 – FEELINGS AND FAITHFULNESS
Make a list of Bible verses that you can turn to when life gets tough. Keep it in your Bible to remind you to "preach to yourself". Perhaps use a prayer journal or diary to help you. (The book of 1 Peter is a great place to start.)

71 – SAUL SUMMONS SAMUEL'S SPIRIT
Saul still stubbornly refused to submit to God's will and yet again thought he could manipulate God. For that rejection of God, punishment would come. Fast (v19). That's next in 1 Samuel.

Read Mark 15 v 34
Jesus faced being abandoned by His Father and took all His anger upon Himself so that we wouldn't have to. Take some time to let that really sink in and then thank Him.

72 – TRAPPED AGAIN?
It wasn't exactly a great plan to hang out in the land of the Philistines, but looking back over these chapters, can you see how God has quietly taken care of David despite his unwise decision? Thank the Lord that His plans are greater than ours and we cannot ultimately mess them up.

73 – RETURN TO TRAGEDY
Holding back from personal revenge when we are hurt or angry is hard.
Read 1 Peter 2 v 21–25
▶ *What did Jesus suffer?*
▶ *Why could He trust God?*
▶ *What should our response be?*

74 – RESCUE MISSION
Read Colossians 1 v 13–14
Spend some time thinking about how Jesus rescues us from darkness. Then go on to read verses 15–20 and reflect on what a mighty king Jesus is.

▷ *Which verse will you particularly take with you into the rest of the week?*

75 – END OF PART ONE
1 Samuel seems to end on a downer. But God hadn't left His people without a leader. David would take on the role. But for David, being God's chosen one hadn't been a passport to an easy life.

▷ *How do we see that same truth in Jesus?*

▷ *What's the reminder here for those of us who follow God's chosen King?*

ISAIAH

76 – GOD'S PERFECT CITY
Read verse 6 again, and then Matthew 26 v 67 and 27 v 26–31

▷ *What do you want to say to Jesus right now?*

Read Isaiah 50 v 8–9, then Romans 8 v 31–39

▷ *Why shouldn't Christians worry about opposition? (v31–33)*

▷ *Where is Jesus now and what is He doing? (v34)*

▷ *What should Christians expect in this life? (v36)*

▷ *But who can separate them from God? (v35)*

▷ *What can take eternal life away from them? (v38–39)*

77 – HERE'S THE GOOD NEWS
Read verse 1 again
God's true people are those who have a personal relationship with Him which leads to holiness of life.

By the way, Rahab in v9 isn't the same Rahab who helped God's spies in Joshua chapter 2. It is Isaiah's nickname for Egypt and means "big mouth".

78 – YOU SNOOZE, YOU LOSE
Read Isaiah 52 v 11 and then 2 Corinthians 6 v 14 – 7 v 1

▷ *What words can answer the questions of v14–16?*

▷ *How should God's people behave? (7 v 1)*

▷ *Why? (6 v 18)*

Paul was telling the believers of Corinth to have nothing to do with the city's idols. God is enough — serve Him only. For us, he's *not* saying: "Don't be friends with non-believers." But he *is* saying: "Don't fall for their gods — the things they value more than God".

▷ *How do you get too involved with "worldly" stuff?*

▷ *What do you need to run away from?*

80 – A LIFE FOR OUR LIVES
Read Leviticus 16 v 20–22 and Isaiah 53 v 4–6
The big idea here is substitution. It's

the heart of the gospel: Jesus dying in our place, standing in for us, being our substitute. Next time you talk to someone about Jesus, will you make sure you explain about Him dying for us?

How do we know Isaiah 53 is talking about Jesus? Check these out:
Acts 8 v 26–40, Luke 22 v 37
1 Peter 2 v 22, Philippians 2 v 5–11

81 – SINGING PRACTICE
Read verses 1–3 and 9–10
We're reminded of God's promises...
to Abraham: **Genesis 12 v 1–3, 7**
　　　　　　Genesis 18 v 13–14
to Moses: **Exodus 19 v 4–6**
to Noah (and all humanity):
Genesis 9 v 12–17.
These promises were still in force and are fulfilled in the work of Jesus!

82 – FEAST YOUR EYES ON THIS
Read verses 1–3 again
The response to God rescuing us is to "hear" and "come". Sounds simple. So why do we make it hard?

Read verses 6–7
Did you notice what hearing and coming will involve?
• Seek the Lord
• Call on His name
• Forsake/abandon wicked ways
• Turn to the Lord.
▷ *Think how you can use these four steps to describe how to become a Christian and how to carry on as one.*

83 – WAIT WATCHING
Read verses 1–2 again
Here's how Barry Webb explains it: *"The fact that maintaining justice is so closely linked to keeping the Sabbath may surprise us, but it would not surprise any Israelites in Old Testament times. The Sabbath was about rest; not just for masters, but also for servants, foreigners and even working animals. To keep the Sabbath showed that you served the God who created the world and cared for everyone and everything in it. The Sabbath rest was a sign of the final rest which all God's people will enjoy in the new heavens and new earth (Isaiah 66 v 22–23). So Israelites keeping the Sabbath was a sign that the whole of life was to be lived in submission to God, and that meant sharing His concern for justice."* More on the Sabbath thing on day 85.

84 – BEASTLY LEADERS
Read Isaiah 56 v 11
then Ezekiel chapter 34
▷ *What crimes had Israel's leaders (shepherds) committed? (v2–6)*
▷ *What were the consequences? (v10)*
▷ *So what did God promise for His people (sheep)? (v11–16)*
▷ *What would God's rescuing of His people also involve? (v17)*
▷ *What further promises did God give? (v23–24)*

God gathering His people meant weeding out any who'd never obeyed Him (v18–19). And God would raise up another David, a servant of God, to rule and care for His true people. That's Jesus.

86 – PAYBACK TIME
Read verse 17
and then Ephesians 6 v 14–17
The way to stand in battle against spiritual opposition is to rely fully on God and His all-conquering resources.

▷ *How does that apply to you in specific battles you face?*

87 – FUTURE PERFECT
Throughout his huge book, Isaiah has been slowly building up a picture of God's eternal city. Check out these verses for what we know so far:
Isaiah 2 v 2–4; 4 v 2–6; 25 v 6–10; 26 v 1–6; 35 v 1–10; 60 v 14–21

"Redeemer" = the one who shoulders all the needs of a close relative. Read verse 16 again and think:

▷ *What is it that we'll fully appreciate at this future time?*
▷ *What will it be like to know God like this?*
▷ *What effect should this anticipation have on us now?*

88 – FANTASTIC FUTURE
Read verses 1–3 again
Jesus didn't come to give people on below-average incomes a better life or to break prisoners out of jail. Nope. Essentially, it's picture language that Isaiah has been using all along to describe how *poor* we are without God and how, without Him, we're *prisoners* of sin and

the devil. Jesus brings us eternal riches and releases us from slavery to sin!

89 – LISTEN UP!
A reminder of the big picture in Isaiah: Chapters 1–37 introduced us to the perfect King who would reign for ever. Chapters 38–55 showed us the suffering Servant who would save His people. Chapters 56–66 brought us the conquering Hero who would return to wrap up God's salvation and judgment. And all three figures are combined in Jesus. Wow!

90 – PUNISHMENT AND PRAISE
Today's slice of Isaiah is up there with the best prayers of the Bible. Take your time to look over it again. And think:

▷ *What did Isaiah make sure to remember about God before he started asking?*
▷ *What's the lesson here for us?*
▷ *How should a knowledge of God's character and promises change the way we pray?*
▷ *Why is it good to be totally honest, like Isaiah, as we pray?*

Read Isaiah 63 v 10, 11, 14
The Spirit is mentioned here quite a bit. These verses show He's personal (can be grieved), is holy, is the Spirit of the Lord, and is the one who carries out God's care of His people.

engage wants to hear from YOU!

▶ Share experiences of God at work in your life
▶ Any questions you have about the Bible or the Christian life?
▶ How can we make *engage* better?

Email us — **martin@thegoodbook.co.uk**

Or send us a letter/postcard/cartoon/sandwich to:

engage 37 Elm Road, New Malden, Surrey, KT3 3HB, UK

In the next engage

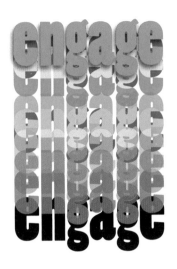

Revelation Jesus wins!
Matthew The big picture
2 Samuel Kingdom come
Obadiah Ob-scure prophet
Plus: Homosexuality: what the Bible says
Overview of the Bible
Why do I keep sinning?
What on earth is sanctification?

Order engage now!

Make sure you order the next issue of **engage**. Or even better, grab a one-year subscription to make sure **engage** lands in your hands as soon as it's out.

Call us to order in the UK on **0333 123 0880**
International: **+44 (0) 20 8942 0880**

or visit your friendly neighbourhood website:
UK: www.thegoodbook.co.uk
N America: www.thegoodbook.com
Australia: www.thegoodbook.com.au
New Zealand: www.thegoodbook.co.nz